## *Taking the Earth for Fou*

This book is designed for the reader who wants to study the deeper significant principles of the ritual magic of the Hermetic Order of the Golden Dawn, possibly the most famous such order the world has known. The authors take you through the steps of waiting in the antechamber as you anticipate going through the Zelator Grade ceremony. The first steps into the grade are shown, as well as how and why the ritualistic process unfolds. The authors share some first-hand experiences of those who have undergone this ritual and tell you what to expect, giving you a study guideline to go with it.

Until recently, books about the Golden Dawn were not written by initiates of any legitimate temple (with the exception of Israel Regardie). Pat and Chris Zalewski take you deep into the hidden mysteries of the Golden Dawn from the viewpoint of one of its highest initiates. For those who want to study ritual magic in a group, this book takes you through the processes with firm guidelines of the dos and don'ts of Hermetic ritual. It was written to help those in existing Golden Dawn temples explain previously unpublished teachings of the Order. For individuals who wish to utilize magic in the privacy of their own homes, this book is a must in the sense that it teaches you about magic, including the traps and shortcuts that can be applied on a solo basis.

Nothing has been published on the Zelator ritual before now, and this unique book reveals the whole concept of Golden Dawn symbols and prompts that the candidate must go through before admission to the Grade of Zelator. The Zelator Grade is one where the postulant has his aura magnetically earthed and wherein the physical body is revitalized. In the previous book in this series, the reader was shown the whole process of first initiation. Now things are taken a step further as the candidate embraces the forces of the Earth element and its effects.

## About the Authors

Pat and Chris Zalewski live in Wellington, New Zealand, where they are co-chiefs of the Golden Dawn Temple, Thoth-Hermes. Both were initiated and instructed in the Golden Dawn teachings by ex-members of the New Zealand temple Whare Ra, which was founded in 1912 and closed in 1978. Both are keen astrologers and have a strong interest in Wiccancraft and the study of comparative religions. They have written a number of books together on the Golden Dawn theme.

## To Write to the Authors

We cannot guarantee that every letter written to the authors can be answered, but all will be forwarded. Both the authors and the publisher appreciate hearing from readers, learning of your enjoyment and benefit from this book. Llewellyn also publishes a bi-monthly news magazine with news and reviews of practical esoteric studies and articles helpful to the student. Some readers' questions and comments to the authors may be answered through this magazine's columns if permission to do so is included in the original letter. The authors sometimes participate in seminars and workshops, and dates and places are announced in *The Llewellyn New Times*. For more information about the Golden Dawn or to ask a question write to:

Ra-Horakhty Temple, Hermetic Society of the Golden Dawn
31849 Pacific Highway South, Suite 107
Federal Way, Washington 98003

To write to the authors, address:

Pat & Chris Zalewski
c/o LLEWELLYN PUBLICATIONS
P.O. Box 64383-896, St. Paul, MN 55164-0383, U.S.A.
Please enclosed a self-addressed, stamped envelope for reply, or $1.00 to cover costs.

LLEWELLYN'S GOLDEN DAWN SERIES

# Z-5
# Secret Teachings of the Golden Dawn

## Book II
## The Zelator Ritual
## 1=10

### Pat and Chris Zalewski

1992
Llewellyn Publications
St. Paul, Minnesota 55164-0383, U.S.A.

FIRST EDITION

Illustrations by Richard Dudschus and David Stoelk
Photography by Nikolaj C. Bell

Library of Congress Cataloging-in-Publication Data
Zalewski, Pat, 1948-
    Z-5 : secret teachings of the Golden Dawn.
    (Llewellyn's Golden Dawn series)
    Contents: bk. 1. The neophyte ritual, 0=0 — bk. 2. The zelator ritual,
        1=10 / by Pat and Chris Zalewski.
    1. Hermetic Order of the Golden Dawn—Rituals.    I. Zalewski, Chris.
    II. Title.    III. Title: Z five.    IV. Series.
    BF1623.R7Z34    1991            135'.4                        90-26728
    ISBN 0-87542-897-5 (v. 1)
    ISBN 0-87542-896-7 (v. 2)

Llewellyn Publications
A Division of Llewellyn Worldwide, Ltd.
P.O. Box 64383, St. Paul, MN 55164-0383

# ABOUT LLEWELLYN'S GOLDEN DAWN SERIES

Just as, 100 years ago, the original Order of the Golden Dawn *initiated* a powerful rebirth of interest in The Western Esoteric Tradition that has lasted through this day, so do we expect this series of books of add new impetus to The Great Work itself among an ever broadening base of sincere students.

> *I further promise and swear that with the Divine Permission, I will from this day forward, apply myself to the Great Work—which is: to purify and exalt my Spiritual Nature so that with the Divine Aid I may at length attain to be more than human, and thus gradually raise and unite myself to my Higher and Divine Genius, and that in this event I will not abuse the great power entrusted to me.*

With this oath, the Adeptus Minor of the Inner Order committed him/herself to undertake, consciously and deliberately, that which was ordained as the birthright of all Humanity: TO BECOME MORE THAN HUMAN!

It is this that is the ultimate message of Esotericism: that evolution continues, and that the purpose of each life is to grow into the Image set for us by our Creator: to attain and reveal our own Divinity.

These books and tapes will themselves make more easily accessible the Spiritual Technology that is inherent in the Golden Dawn System. It is a system that allows for individual as well as group endeavor; a system that works within or without an organized lodge; a system that is based on universal principles that will be shown to be global in their impact today.

And it is practical. The works in this series will be practical in their application. You need neither travel to the Mountain Top nor obtain any tool other than your own Consciousness. No garment need you other than that of your own Imagination. No authority need you other than that of your own True Will.

Set forth, then, into The New Dawn—a New Start on the greatest adventure there is: to become One with the Divine Genius.

**Other Books by Pat Zalewski and Chris Zalewski**

*The Secret Inner Order Rituals of the Golden Dawn*
(Falcon Press, 1988)

*Herbs in Magic & Alchemy* (by Chris Zalewski)
(Prism Press, 1990)

*Golden Dawn Enochian Magic*
(Llewellyn Publications, 1990)

*Z-5: Secret Teachings of the Golden Dawn*
*Book I: The Neophyte Ritual 0=0*
(Llewellyn Publications, 1991)

*Equinox and Solstice Rituals of the Golden Dawn*
(Llewellyn Publications, 1992)


**Forthcoming from Llewellyn**

*Enochian Chess* (by Chris Zalewski)

*The Kabbalah of the Golden Dawn*

# Contents

# Foreword

This book continues an elucidation of the Golden Dawn system of magic that began with the Zalewskis' previous book on the Neophyte grade (Z-5. Book 1). At this stage the student begins to investigate the four elements (earth, air, water, and fire) beginning with earth. It is the task of the student during this phase of the knowledge search to established the qualities of earth in the worlds of the Kabbalah: What is earth on the material plane? My body is earth—what does that feel like . . . what does that mean to me? How does emotion exhibit the qualities of earth? How does wind erode mountains? What's the similarity? The basin of the ocean is earth; what part of myself contains, restrains and forms the shape and movement of my thoughts? Without a base upon which to lay fuel a fire will burn but fitfully, in what ways do I ground my inspiration in concrete activity?

The objective of the Zelator ceremony is the ritual placement of the earth element into the aura of consciousness of the aspirant. In the ensuing months the student must then become acquainted with the element: learning to identify this element no matter where or how it appears in their subsequent working. The explanatory supplement facilitates the student's exploratory work of the ritual in that it serves to establish associations in the student's mind. It will also inform them of the process whereby these symbol associations may be brought to life within the student.

It is vitally important that the student "do" the independent rituals (ritual of pentagrams, Rose Cross, Invocation, etc.). It is vitally important that the student "do," **beyond a shadow of a doubt,** the work of establishing the earth and subsequent elements in their consciousness. It is vitally important that the student work at establishing and maintaining a relationship with a peer or lover. They are no different—relationships are initiated, developed and maintained only by careful attention and response to the needs expressed by the partners in the relationship. And again, like any other relationship, expression of needs facilitates response by the other partner whether physical or non-physical. The Zelator, then, must ask her/himself what does earth need from them (physically, emotionally, mentally, spiritually). If the student has reasonable command of imagination they may visualize Gnomes and engage in conversation regarding these needs (being ever wary of getting one's own "stuff" in the way; i.e., hearing what you want to hear). The student will be able to engage in meaningful dialogue with the elemental as a result of this interchange based in equality.

Changing oneself is no piece of cake, the answers to these questions may be difficult to accept and integrate into the personality of the student magician but through diligence and persistence change will occur. Yes, the prime ingredient to ritual is to do it. The prime ingredient to instituting change in the magician is to work at it—to do it.

*—Fra. K∴ M∴ T∴*
***Hermetic Society of the Golden Dawn***

# Introduction

This book is the second in the series of Golden Dawn ritual analyses and is the first on the elemental grades. Very little if anything has been done on the elemental ceremonies in the past, because their function has, for the most part, been obscure. Most Golden Dawn students seem to consider that exposure to the elemental Tablets is the main pinnacle of these ceremonies, and some have even substituted the "Opening by Watchtower" for these grades.

The operative word, throughout both the Outer and Inner Order of the Golden Dawn, was "fusion," where all the main systems were brought together for combined usage. While it is true that the Elemental Tablets (or Watchtowers, as they are sometimes called) *were* the pinnacle, and related various subsystems together, it is equally true that these tablets were an impetus or force *behind* the system and were never envisaged for direct use in the Outer Order. To truly understand the function of the elemental grades, you must go through the ceremonies.

This book is an analysis of the 1=10 Ritual, from the New Zealand Whare Ra Temple. Part 1 is the ritual itself. The sec-

ond part is an analysis of the ritual which includes many of the
"word of mouth" teachings of both the Golden Dawn and, later,
the Stella Matutina. Part 3 gives an analysis of the 1-10 Grade
from the Whare Ra Temple, though its actual origin is obscure.
The writing style is too erratic for R. W. Felkin, who founded
and headed the temple, but reminds me very much of Ms.
Felkin. The whole lecture gives a very Christian slant to the ritual. Overall, however, it has quite a few pearls of wisdom in it
and should be studied with this concept in mind.

This lecture was usually read to the Zelator or Zelators
directly after the ceremony, before any officers had a chance to
leave the temple. Originally, we thought of blending together
this analysis with our own, but, due to differences in the writing
style, we decided to leave this version intact, as it was presented to every 1=10 initiate that went through Whare Ra.

This analysis is followed by a series of lectures that were
handed out to the Zelator, also from Whare Ra. For the most
part, this is new ground. Apart from the ritual itself, most of
this material has never been published before.

Part 4 gives A. E. Waite's version of the 1=10 Ritual, plus the
Allocution (explanation) of the ritual. This material was taken
from a set of papers that Waite gave Felkin, though the rituals
themselves are dated 1910 and are Golden Dawn in essence and
format, with only some of the wording of the speeches being different. This is of some importance, for it shows that Waite was
still using the Golden Dawn rituals as late as 1910. Also, his
curious style deserves some airing and is not to be dismissed
lightly.

Although the changes in Waite's ritual were made for the
sake of change, it is evident that the entire structure is still
based on the arrangement of the cipher manuscripts by
MacGregor Mathers. A careful study of this ceremony shows
clearly that it generates just as much power as did the original
Golden Dawn 1=10 ritual. Waite was greatly respected by members of the Golden Dawn, and his knowledge was second only to
that of William Wynn Westcott and Mathers (according to
Felkin, who by his own admission was jealous of Waite). Waite's

books on Paracelsus and the kabbalah (qabalah) show an understanding of both alchemy and the kabbalah that very few in the Golden Dawn possessed.

We cannot overemphasize the importance of participating in, or going through, the elemental grade ceremonies. The 1=10 Ceremony is something of an enigma, for it differs a great deal from the other three elemental rituals, in the sense of magical direction. Its main concern is strengthening both the physical and astral body of the Zelator. It is not associated with any planet except the one we live on. It fuses together a number of very important magical techniques, such as auric alchemy, the magical use of biblical Psalms, and the magical use of the *Sepher Yetzirah*. Through the diagrams on the altar and the walls, it draws from the energy of the ancient Temple of Solomon. This creates an empathy with the Earth Tablets.

The candidate is introduced to various god-forms on the Tree of Life; he will later utilize and command these in the higher levels. His advanced work will include skrying the Enochian pyramids, Enochian Chess, talismanic work, and other aspects of the Z.2 formula that the adept must utilize in the Inner Order. All of this is absorbed at a basic level by the Zelator, either directly or indirectly, but absorbed nevertheless, and is resurrected at a later level of the Order's work. It formulates a base on which to work, when one begins to work, directly, with the planetary energies.

Previous publications concerning the Golden Dawn have had a number of diagrams missing from the rituals, as well as many associated commentaries for each of the grades, even though these rituals were Golden Dawn originals. To remedy this, we have written the Z-5 series of books on both the rituals and commentaries of the Golden Dawn, from Neophyte to Adeptus Exemptus.

It has long been the assumption that the rituals of the Stella Matutina were watered-down versions of those of the Golden Dawn. This assumption was mainly due to the papers of the English temples being altered, though those in the New Zealand Order were, for the most part, identical to those of the

Golden Dawn temples, and, in some instances, included additional information.

The various diagrams presented to the candidate as he or she goes through the elemental rituals have a very specific purpose. When Whare Ra Temple was first established, a number of classes were held by Felkin. These went into specific detail about the diagrams. We were told that this was the way of teaching in the Isis-Urania Temple during the heyday of the Order prior to 1900. So, instead of just seeing a diagram on the wall during the ritual, the students were taken by their respective teachers through an entire sequence of related information at a later stage.

This practice, however, fell in abeyance in most temples after 1900, and the diagrams, once an elaborate method of study, represented a small piece of information. Judging by the later unpublished lectures of Mathers, it appears that he intended to include some of the diagrams from the 1=10 grade in his Enochian lectures for the Practicus Adeptus Minor Grade.

Both Aleister Crowley (in *The Equinox*) and Israel Regardie (in *The Complete Golden Dawn System of Magic*) did not think much of the elemental rituals. We have different opinions on this subject, mainly due to the fact that the person who put us through the grades, Jack Taylor, was an esoteric genius who had a magical power and perception I have not perceived in any other person. He knew what he was doing. Crowley told Regardie how unimpressed he was with the elemental grades, while Regardie came to the same conclusion, though both had little regard for their respective Hierophants during these rituals.

Taylor, on the other hand, could cradle your aura and introduce you to energies on one level at a time. When he showed a diagram during ritual, he would open up even more currents of energy, so that one could experience a small manifestation of what it represented. Very few people could do this—virtually none in the Golden Dawn or the Stella Matutina. If there were any who had this ability, you could probably count their numbers on the fingers of one hand.

Regardie, at dinner one night with an American temple chief

visiting in New Zealand, argued that, on the one hand, the elemental grades were unnecessary, yet, on the other hand, they were effective in opening up the aura and inflating the ego. To understand his viewpoint, you would have had to know Regardie. Taylor, however, had such abilities that many held him in awe and others feared him. He had reached the point where, when he was talking about the effectiveness of the Earth grade, he would pull these energies out of his own aura and show what he was talking about by the "show me, don't tell me" principle.

One of the let-downs within the Order was the fact that those who acted as Hierophant did not often have the same ability at ritual as people such as Taylor, Mathers, Felkin, or Waite. Although following the teachings, many unfortunately could not muster the important internal combination that every Hierophant should possess, and as a result their ritual initiations were far short of what they should have been. Mathers realized this, and while he knew he could show them the way, he could not give them the internal impetus to go with it. It's a pity that Crowley and Regardie did not have adequate Hierophants, for if they had, I am sure they would have felt the true power of the elemental ceremonies.

Taylor felt that the 5=6 grade (Adeptus Minor) was not sufficient to be a Hierophant, even though the adept had to undergo training under the Past Hierophant. This was originally done in some temples, but the practice fell into abeyance. The only remaining training was a mechanical approach to ritual that was nothing more than an empty shell. Training a Hierophant takes many years.

We have often thought that temples that are large enough should have classes to train prospective Hierophants. The students should be graded on knowledge and ability. Anyone who failed to pass should not be allowed to hold the Hierophant's position.

When people, both within and without the Order, start talking about shortcuts such as skipping the elemental grades, we are reminded of the story on the formation of the golem of

Prague. Rabbi Yehuda ben Bezalel (Maharal) could have saved himself a lot of trouble in bringing life to the golem if he had not used the elements—or could he?

One of the recent buzzwords used by Golden Dawn aspirants, and unfortunately by some Chiefs, is "conceptionalize"—which should read "cop-out." This approach is generally advocated by those armchair magicians who talk instead of doing. Some of them would have us change the Golden Dawn system into sitting back and visualizing the whole ritual procedure. These people are either too lazy or do not have the ability to perform Golden Dawn ritual. They think that Will alone will suffice, which it will not. The prime ingredient of ritual is to get out there and do it, not just sit back and theorize about it.

The commentary and explanations of the Z-5, Books 2-4 (the 1=10 to the 4=7 grades), were originally a series of four lectures that were part of the 6=5 grade teachings (the explanations of the Portal and 5=6 being part of the 7=4 grade) of the Thoth-Hermes Temple. I have taken the liberty of expanding these somewhat and adding in the Outer Order study program with them.

—Pat and Chris Zalewski
New Zealand, 1988

# Part 1

# The Ritual

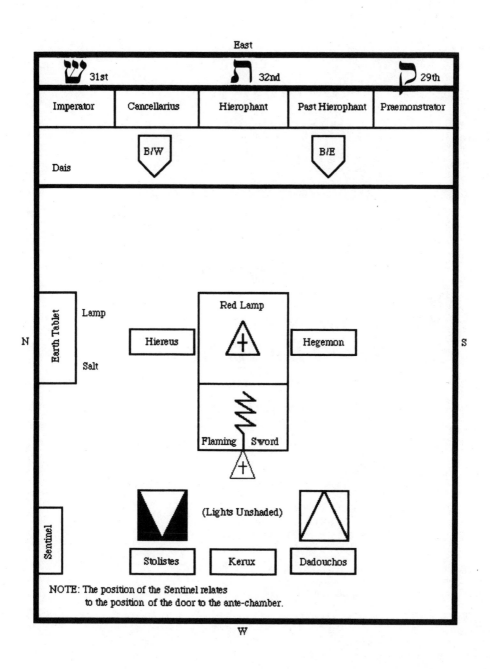

*Temple Arrangement—First Part*

# Ceremony of the
# 1=10 Grade of Zelator

## *Officers*

On the dais: Imperator, Cancellarius, Praemonstrator, Past Hierophant, Hierophant
(The first four of these officers are optional at this point.)

In the hall: Hiereus, Hegemon, Kerux, Stolistes, Dadouchos, Sentinel

## *Requirements*

Hoodwink, Sash, Fylfot Cross, Three Portals, Shewbread Diagram, Candlestick Diagram, Altar of Incense Diagram, Triangle Diagram, Diagram on Altar, Earth Tablet.

*Note:* If this ceremony is the first to be performed at any meeting, the regulation with regard to the use of the Lesser Ritual of the Pentagram and the prayer to the East holds good, as laid down in the rubric of the 0=0 Grade.

## *Opening*

The members being assembled and robed, and seated each in his/her proper place:

Hiereus: (Gives one knock)

Hierophant: *Fraters and Sorores of the 1=10 Grade of the Stella Matutina, assist me to open the temple in the Grade of Zelator. Frater (Soror) Kerux, see that the Temple is properly guarded.*

(Kerux knocks without opening door. Sentinel replies with one knock.)

Kerux: *Very Honored Hierophant, the Temple is properly guarded.*

Hierophant: *Honored Hiereus, see that none below the Grade of Zelator is present.*

Hiereus: *Fraters et Sorores, give the sign of the 1=10.*

(All give the signs of Zelator. Hiereus gives sign.)

Hiereus: *Very Honored Hierophant, no one below the Grade of Zelator is present.*

(Hierophant gives sign.)

Hierophant: *Purify and consecrate the Temple with Water and Fire.*

(Kerux advances between the Pillars. Stolistes and Dadouchos, one each side of the Pillars, advance to center of the hall. All salute. Dadouchos makes a cross in the air with the censer and swings it forward three times.)

Dadouchos: *I consecrate with Fire.*

(Stolistes makes a cross with cup and sprinkles thrice towards the East while saying:)

Stolistes: *I purify with Water.*

Kerux: *The Temple is cleansed.*

(All salute; all three retire, Kerux leading and passing with Sol.)

Hierophant: *Let the Element of this Grade be named that it may be awakened in the spheres of those and in the sphere of the Order.*

Hegemon: *The Element of Earth.*

(Hiereus gives one knock.)

Hiereus: *Let us adore the Lord and King of the Earth.*

(All face East.)

Hierophant: *Adonai Ha Aretz. Adonai Melekh! Unto Thee be the Kingdom, the Power* (makes a circle) *and the Glory. Malkuth* (makes a cross), *Geburah, Gedulah.*

(Hierophant makes a circle and cross with scepter before him.)

*The Rose of Sharon and the Lily of the Valley. Amen.*

(All give Zelator Sign. Kerux goes to North and sprinkles salt before the Tablet while saying:)

Kerux: *Let the Earth adore Adonai.*

(Hierophant leaves his/her place and goes to North. S/he stands facing the center of the Tablet of the North, and at a convenient distance therefrom [see diagram, page 70]. Hiereus takes his/her place at the right side of Hierophant, Hegemon on the left side of Hierophant, Stolistes and Dadouchos behind Hegemon. All officers face North. Hierophant makes Invoking Pentagram of Earth in the air in front of, and concentric with, the Tablet of the North, saying:)

Hierophant: *And the Elohim said, "Let us make Adam in Our Image, after our likeness let him have dominion over the fish of the sea and over the fowl of the air and over the cattle and over all of the Earth and over every creeping thing that creepeth over the Earth."*

*And Elohim created Eth ha Adam in their own Image, in the Image of Elohim created they them. In the name of Adonai Melekh and of the Bride and Queen of the Kingdom, Spirits of Earth adore Adonai!*

(Hierophant hands his scepter to Hiereus, and taking sword makes the Sign of the Ox in the center of the pentagram, saying:)

Hierophant: *In the Name of Auriel, the Great Archangel of Earth, and by the sign of the Head of the Ox, Spirits of Earth, Adore Adonai!*

(Hierophant returns sword to Hiereus then takes miter-headed scepter from Hegemon and makes a cross in the air, saying:)

Hierophant: *In the Names and Letters of the Great Northern Quadrangle, Spirits of Earth, adore Adonai!*

(Hierophant returns scepter to Hegemon and takes the cup from Stolistes, makes a cross, and sprinkles thrice to the North, saying:)

Hierophant: *In the Three Great Secret Names of God borne upon the Banners of the North—EMOR DIAL HECTEGA—Spirits of Earth, adore Adonai!*

(Hierophant returns cup to Stolistes and takes censer from Dadouchos, makes a cross and three forward swings, and says:)

Hierophant: *In the Name of IC ZOD HEH CHAL, Great King of the North, Spirits of Earth adore Adonai!*

(Hierophant returns censer to Dadouchos and, taking back scepter from Hiereus, returns to Throne. All officers return to their places by way of Sol. All members face as usual.)

Hierophant: (Knocks four times, knocks three times, then knocks three more times)

Hegemon: (Knocks four times, knocks three times, then knocks three more times)

Hiereus: (Knocks four times, knocks three times, then knocks three more times)

## *Advancement: First Part*

(Hierophant sits East of Altar. Hiereus sits North of Altar. Hegemon sits South of Altar.)

Hierophant: *Fraters and Sorores, our Frater (Soror), having made such progress in the Paths of the Occult Science as has enabled him/her to pass an examination in the required knowledge, is now eligible for advancement to this Grade, and I have duly received a dispensation from the Greatly Honored Chiefs of the Second Order to admit him (her) in due form. Honored Hegemon, superintend the preparation of the Neophyte and give the customary alarm.*

(Hegemon salutes with 1=10 sign, and leaves the room by South and West. Sentinel prepares Neophyte, who wears sash of 0=0 Grade and is blindfolded. S/he carries a Fylfot Cross in his/her right hand. Hegemon instructs Neophyte in the knocks of the Grade. Kerux opens the door until it is just ajar.)

Hegemon: *Let me enter the Portal of Wisdom.*

Kerux: *I will.*

(Kerux opens door and lets them in. Sentinel turns down lights.)

Hierophant: *Except Adonai build the house, their labor is but lost that build it. Except Adonai keep the city, the watchman waketh in vain. Frater (Soror) Neophyte, by what aid dost thou seek admission to the 1=10 grade of the Stella Matutina?*

(Hegemon answers for Neophyte.)

Hegemon: *By the guidance of Adonai; by the possession of the necessary knowledge; by the dispensation of the Greatly Honored Chiefs of the Second Order; by the signs and token of the 1=10 Grade: by this symbol of the Hermetic Cross.*

(Kerux takes cross from Hegemon.)

Hierophant: *Give the step and signs of the Neophyte.*

(Neophyte gives them)

Hierophant: *Frater Kerux, receive from the Neophyte the Token, Grand Word, and Password of the 0=0 Grade.*

(Kerux places himself in front of Neophyte.)

Kerux: *Give me the Grip of the Neophyte.*

(Neophyte gives Grip.)

Kerux: *Give me the Word.*

(Neophyte gives Word.)

Kerux: *Give me the Password.*

(Neophyte gives Password. Kerux turns to Hierophant and gives Grade salute.)

Kerux: *Very Honored Hierophant, I have received them.*

(Hierophant instructs Hegemon.)

Hierophant: *Lead the Neophyte to the West and set him/her between the Mystic Pillars, with his/her face towards the East.*

(Hegemon places Neophyte between the Pillars.)

Hierophant: *Frater (Soror) _____, will you pledge yourself to maintain the same secrecy regarding the Mysteries of this Grade as you are pledged to maintain regarding those of the 0=0 Grade—never to reveal them to the world, and not to even confer them upon a Neophyte, without a dispensation from the Greatly Honored Chiefs of the Second Order?*

Neophyte: *I will.*

Hierophant: *Then you will kneel on both your knees, lay your right hand on the ground, and say: "I swear by the Earth whereon I kneel."*

(Neophyte makes pledge.)

Hierophant: *Let the symbol of blindness be removed.*

(Hegemon unbinds Neophyte's eyes. Sentinel turns up lights. Hegemon goes back to his/her proper place. Neophyte remains kneeling between Pillars with his/her hand on the ground. Kerux takes the salt from before the Tablet of the North and, passing round the Altar with Sol, stands in front of Neophyte, facing him/her, and holding the salt in front of him/her.)

Kerux: *Take salt with your left hand and cast it to the North; saying: "Let the Powers of Earth witness my pledge."*

(Neophyte makes pledge. Kerux replaces salt, and returns to his/her place.)

Hierophant: *Let the Neophyte rise and let him/her be purified with Water and consecrated with Fire, in confirmation of his/her pledge, and in the Name of the Lord of the Universe who works in silence and whom naught but silence can express.*

(Dadouchos comes forward, around South Pillar, stands before Neophyte, and makes a cross and three forward swings of the censer, saying:)

Dadouchos: *In the name of the Lord of the Universe, who works in silence and whom naught but silence can express, I consecrate thee with Fire.*

(Dadouchos returns by the way s/he came. Stolistes comes round North Pillar, stands before Neophyte, makes cross on forehead, and sprinkles thrice, saying:)

Stolistes: *In the name of the Lord of the Universe, who works in silence and whom naught but silence can express, I purify thee with Water.*

(Stolistes returns to place as s/he came.)

Hierophant: *The 1=10 Grade of Zelator is a preparation for other Grades, a threshold before our discipline, and it shows by its imagery, the Light of the Hidden Knowledge dawning in Darkness of Creation; and you are now to begin to analyze and comprehend the Nature of the Light. To this end, you stand between the Pillars, in the Gateway where the secrets of the 0=0 Grade were communicated to you.*

    *Prepare to enter the immeasurable regions.*

    *"And Tetragrammaton Elohim planted a Garden Eastward in Eden, and out of the ground made Tetragrammaton Elohim to grow every tree that is pleasant to the sight and good for food; the Tree of Life also, in the midst of the Garden, and the Tree of Knowledge of Good and of Evil." This is the Tree that has two Paths, and it is the tenth Sephirah, Malkuth, and it has about it seven columns, and the Four Splendors whirl around it a vision of the Mercabah of Ezekiel; and from Gedulah it drives an influx of mercy, and from Geburah it drives an influx of severity, and the Tree of Knowledge of Good and of Evil shall it be until it is united with Supernals in Daath. But the Good which is under it is the Archangel Metatron, and the Evil is called the Archangel Samael, and between them lies the straight and narrow way, where the Archangel Sandalphon keeps watch. The souls and the angels are above its branches, and the qlippoth or demons dwell under its roots.*

    *Let the Neophyte enter the Pathway of Evil.*

(Kerux takes his place in front of Neophyte, leads him/her in a northeast direction towards the Hiereus, halts and steps out of the direct line between Hiereus and Neophyte.)

Hiereus: *Whence comest thou?*

Kerux: *I come from between the two Pillars, and I seek the Light of the Hidden Knowledge in the Name of Adonai.*

Hiereus: *And the Great Angel Samael answered, and said: "I am the Prince of Darkness and of Night. The foolish and rebellious gaze upon the face of the created World, and find therein nothing but terror and obscurity. It is to them the terror of Darkness and they are drunken men stumbling in the Darkness. Return, for thou canst not pass me by."*

(Kerux leads Neophyte back as s/he came, to between the Pillars.)

Hierophant: *Let the Neophyte enter the Pathway of Good.*

(Kerux leads Neophyte southeast, and halts opposite Hegemon, stepping aside from before Neophyte.)

Hegemon: *Whence comest thou?*

Kerux: *I come from between the Pillars, and I seek the Light of the Hidden Knowledge in the Name of Adonai.*

Hegemon: *The Great Angel Metatron answered, and said: "I am the Angel of the Presence Divine. The Wise gaze upon the Created World and behold there the dazzling image of the Creator. Not Yet can thine eyes bear that dazzling image of the Creator. Not yet can thine eyes bear that dazzling Image. Return, for thou canst not pass me by."*

(Kerux turns and leads Neophyte back between the Pillars.)

Hierophant: *Let the Neophyte enter the straight and narrow Pathway which turns neither to the right hand nor to the left hand.*

(Kerux leads Neophyte directly up center of hall until s/he is near the Altar and steps aside from before Neophyte, leaving him/her to face the Altar unobstructed. Hiereus and Hegemon speak together:)

Hiereus  
Hegemon } : *Whence comest thou?*

(Hiereus and Hegemon cross scepter and sword before Altar.)

Kerux: *I come from between the Pillars and I seek the Light of the Hidden Knowledge in the Name of Adonai.*

(Hierophant advances to East of the Altar with scepter of Hegemon and, raising it to an angle of 45 degrees, says:)

Hierophant: *But the Great Angel Sandalphon said: "I am the reconciler for Earth, and the Celestial Soul therein. Form is invisible alike in Darkness and in blinding Light. I am the left-hand Kerub of the Ark and the feminine power, as Metatron is the right-hand Kerub and the masculine power, and I prepare the way for the Celestial Light."*

(Hegemon and Hiereus step back to South and North of Altar, respectively. Hierophant takes Neophyte by right hand, with his/her left, and pointing to the Altar and diagram, says:)

Hierophant: *And Tetragrammaton placed Kerubim at the East of the Garden of Eden and a Flaming Sword which turned every way to keep the Path of the Tree of Life, for He has created Nature that Man, being cast out of Eden, may not fall into the Void. He has bound Man with the Stars, as with the chain. He allures him with scattered fragments of the Divine Body in bird and beast and flower, and he laments over him in the Wind and the Sea and in the Birds. When the time is ended, he will call the Kerubim from the East of the Garden, and he shall be consumed and become infinite and holy.*

*Receive now the Secrets of this Grade. The step is thus given: 6 by 6, showing you passed the threshold. The Sign is given by raising the right hand to an angle of 45 degrees. It is the position in which the Hierophant interposed for you between the Hiereus and the Hegemon. The Token is given by grasping fingers, thumb touching thumb, to form a triangle. It refers to the Ten Sephiroth. The Word is Adonai Ha-Aretz, and means Adonai the Lord of the Earth, to which Element this Grade is allotted. The Mystic Number is 55, and from it is formed the Password, Nun Heh. It means Ornament, and when given is lettered separately.*

*The Badge of this Grade is the sash of the Neophyte with the narrow white border, a red cross within the triangle, and the number 1 within a circle and 10 within a square, one on each side of the triangle.*

(Hierophant invests Neophyte with the sash and points out the Three Portals.)

Hierophant: *The Three Portals facing you in the East are the gates of the Paths leading to three further Grades, which, with the Zelator and the Neophyte, form the First and Lowest Order of our Fraternity. Furthermore, they represent the paths which connect the tenth Sephirah, Malkuth, with the other Sephiroth. The letters Tau, Qoph, and Shin make the word Qesheth—a Bow, the reflection of the Rainbow of Promise stretched over our Earth, and which is about the Throne of God.*

(Hierophant resumes Throne. Hegemon points out the Flaming Sword, saying:)

Hegemon: *This drawing of the Flaming Sword of the Kerubim is a representation of the Guardians of the Gates of Eden, just as the Hiereus and Hegemon symbolize the two paths of the Tree of Knowledge of Good and of Evil.*

Hiereus: *In this Grade, the red cross is placed within the white triangle upon the Altar, and it is thus the symbol of the Banner of the West. The triangle refers to the three paths and the cross to the Hidden Knowledge. The cross and the triangle together represent Life and Light.*

(Hierophant points out the Tablet of the North, saying:)

Hierophant: *This Grade is especially referred to the Element of Earth, and therefore one of its principle emblems is the Great Watchtower or Terrestrial Tablet of the North. It is the Third or Great Northern Quadrangle, or Earth Tablet, and it is one of the four Great Tablets of the Elements said to have been given to Enoch by the great Angel Ave. It is*

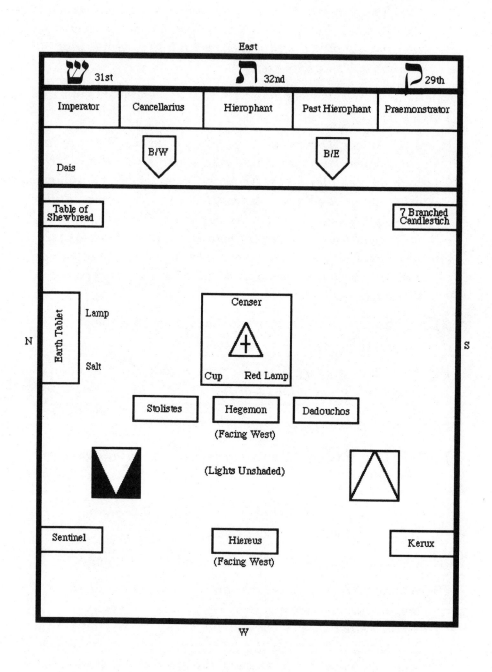

*Temple Arrangement—Second Part*

*divided within itself into four lesser angles. The mystic let-
ters upon it form various divine and angelic Names, in
what our tradition call the Angelic Secret Language. From
it are drawn the Three Holy Secret Names of God, EMOR
DIAL HECTEGA, which are borne upon the Banners of the
North, and there are also numberless name of angels,
archangels, and spirits ruling the element of Earth.*

(Kerux comes forward and hands Fylfot Cross to Hierophant.)

Hierophant: *The Hermetic Cross, which is also called the Fylfot,
Hammer of Thor, and Swastika, is formed of 17 squares out
of a square of 25 lesser squares. These 17 represent the Sun,
the Four Elements, and the Twelve Signs of the Zodiac. In
this Grade, the Lights on the Pillars are unshaded, showing
that you have quitted the Darkness of the Outer World. You
will leave the Temple for a short time.*

(Kerux takes Neophyte out.)

## Second Part

(Temple arranged as in Diagram.)

Hierophant: *Frater (Soror) Kerux, when the Neophyte gives the
proper alarm, you will admit him. Frater(s) (Soror[s])
Stolistes and Dadouchos, assist the Kerux in the reception.*

(Kerux goes out and instructs the Neophyte in the knocks.
Stolistes and Dadouchos take up positions so as to face Neophyte as s/he enters hall. Kerux opens door and admits Neophyte, but does not stand in front of him/her.)

Hierophant: *Frater (Soror) _____, as in the Grade
of Neophyte, you came out of the World to the Gateway of
Hidden Knowledge, so in this Grade you pass through the
Gateway and come into the Holy Place. You are now in the
court of the Tabernacle, where stood the Altar of Burnt Offering, whereon was offered the sacrifices of animals, which
symbolized the Qlippoth, or Evil Demons, who inhabit the*

*plane contiguous to and below the Material Universe.*

(Dadouchos makes a cross in the air with censer and censes Neophyte in silence with three forward swings.)

Hierophant: *Between the Altar and the entrance to the Holy Place stood the Laver of Brass, wherein the priest washed before entering the Tabernacle. It was the symbol of the Waters of Creation.*

(Stolistes makes a cross with water, on Neophyte's forehead and sprinkles thrice in silence.)

Hierophant: *Having made offering at the Altar of Burnt Sacrifice, and having been cleansed at the Laver of Brass, the Priest then entered the Holy Place.*

(Kerux takes Neophyte behind Pillars, to North. Stolistes and Dadouchos return to their places. Hiereus takes his/her stand between the Pillars [Kerux having removed the chair] facing Neophyte. S/he guards the path with his/her sword.)

Hiereus: *Thou canst not pass the gateway which is between the Pillars unless thou canst give the Signs and the Words of the Neophyte.*

(Neophyte gives them and, instructed by the Kerux, advances to a position between the Pillars. Hiereus returns to place in the West. Hegemon comes forward, stands East of Pillars facing Neophyte, and bars the way into the Temple with scepter.)

Hegemon: *Thou canst not enter the Holy Place unless thou canst give the Sign and Grip of the Zelator.*

(Neophyte gives them. Kerux resumes his/her seat, after handing Neophyte over to charge of Hegemon. Hegemon leads Neophyte to the North.)

Hegemon: *To the Northern side of the Holy Table stood the Table of Shewbread. The drawing before you represents its occult meaning. On it, twelve loaves were laid as emblems of the Bread of Life, and it is an image of the Mystery of the Rose of Creation. The twelve circles are the Twelve Signs of the Zodiac, while the lamp in the center is symbolic of the Sun, which is the source of heat and life. The four triangles, whose twelve angles each touch one of the twelve circles, are those of Fire, Earth, Air, and Water, and allude to the four Triplicities of the Zodiac Signs. The triangle inscribed within each of the twelve circles alludes to the three decanates, or phases of ten degrees of each sign. On one side of each triangle is the permutation of Yod Heh Vau Heh which is referred to that particular sign, while on the opposite side of it is the name of one of the Twelve Tribes which are also attributed to it.*

*Now the 22 sounds and letters of the Hebrew alphabet are the foundation of all things. Three Mothers, Seven Double, and Twelve Simple Letters are allotted to the twelve directions in space, and those diverge to infinity and are in the arms of the Eternal. These twelve letters He designed and combined and formed with the twelve celestial constellations of the Zodiac. They are over the Universe as a king traversing his dominions, and they are in the heart of man as a king in warfare.*

*And the Twelve Loaves are the images of those ideas, and are the outer petals of the Rose; while within are the Four Archangels, ruling over the Four Quarters, and the kerubic emblems of the Lion, Man, Bull, and Eagle. Around the great central Lamp, which is an image of the Sun, is the Great Mother of Heaven, symbolized by the letter Heh, the first of the Simple Letters, and by its number five, the pentagram, Malkah the Bride, ruling her Kingdom Malkuth, crowned with a crown of Twelve Stars.*

*These twelve circles further represent the Twelve Foundations of the Holy City of the Apocalypse, while in Christian symbolism the Sun and the Twelve signs are referred to Christ and his Twelve Apostles.*

(Hegemon leads Neophyte to Hiereus, and then returns to place and is seated. Hiereus leads Neophyte to the South.)

Hiereus: *On the Southern side of the Holy Place stood the Seven-Branched Candlestick wherein was burned pure olive oil. It is an Image of the Mystery of Elohim, the Seven Creative Ideas. The symbolic drawing before you represents its occult meaning. The seven circles which surround the heptagram represent the Seven Planets and the Seven Qabbalistic Palaces of Assiah, the Material World, which answer to the Seven Apocalyptic Churches, which are in Asia or Assiah, as these allude to the Seven Lamps before the Throne on another plane.*

*Within each circle is a triangle to represent the Threefold Creative Idea operating in all things. On the right-hand side of each is the Hebrew name of the angel who governs the planet; on the left side is the Hebrew name of the sphere of the planet itself; while the Hebrew letter beneath the base is one of the duplicated letters of the Hebrew alphabet which refers to the Seven Planets.*

*The seven Double Letters of the Hebrew alphabet have each two sounds associated with them, one hard, one soft. They are called "double" because each letter represents a contrary or permutation, thus: Life and Death; Peace and War; Wisdom and Folly; Riches and Poverty; Grace and Indignity; Fertility and Solitude; Power and Servitude.*

*These seven letters point out seven localities: Zenith, Nadir, East, West, North, South, and the Place of the Holiness in the midst sustaining all things. The Archetypal Creator designed, produced, combined, and formed with them the planets of the Universe, the days of the week, and in man, the gate of the soul. He has loved and blessed the number seven more than all things under His Throne. The powers of these seven letters are also shown forth in the Seven Palaces of Assiah, and the seven stars of that vision are the seven archangels who rule them.*

(Hiereus leads Neophyte to Hierophant and returns to place and is seated. Hierophant leads Neophyte to Altar, takes censer from Altar and, holding it with chain short, makes cross and three forward swings.)

Hierophant: *Before the Veil of the Holy of Holies stood the Altar of Incense, of which this Altar is an image. It was of the form of a double cube, thus representing material form as a reflection and duplication of that which is spiritual. The side of the Altar, together with the top and bottom, consists of ten squares, thus symbolizing the Ten Sephiroth, of which the basal one is Malkuth, the realization of the rest upon the material plane, behind which the others are concealed. For were this double cube raised in the air immediately above your head, you would but see the single square forming the lowest side, the others from their positions being concealed from you. Just so, behind the material Universe lies the concealed form of the majesty of God.*

*The Altar of Incense was overlaid with gold to represent the highest degree of purity, but the Altar before you is black to represent the terrestrial Earth. Learn then to separate the pure from the impure, and refine the Gold of the Spirit from the Black Dragon, the corruptible body. Upon the Cubical Altar were Fire, Water, and Incense, the Three Mother Letters of the Hebrew alphabet: Aleph, Mem, and Shin. Mem is silent, Shin is sibilant, and Aleph is the tongue of a balance between these contraries in equilibrium, reconciling and mediating between them. In this is a great mystery, very admirable and recondite. The Fire produced the Heavens, the Water, and the Earth, and the Air is the reconciler between them. In the year, they bring forth the hot, the cold, and the temperate seasons, and in man they are imaged in the head, the chest, and the trunk.*

*I now confer upon you the mystic title of Periclinus (Peri-*

*cline) de Faustis, which signifies that on this Earth you are in a wilderness, far from the Garden of the Happy.*

*    And I give you the symbol of ARETZ, which is the Hebrew name for Earth, to which the 1=10 Grade of Zelator is referred. The word Zelator is derived from the ancient Egyptian Zaruator, signifying, "Searcher of Athor," Goddess of Nature; but others assign it to the meaning of the zealous student, whose first duty was to blow the Athanor of Fire which heated the crucible of the Alchemist.*

(Hierophant resumes seat on the Dais; Kerux leads new Zelator to a seat in the Northwest.)

Hierophant: *Frater Kerux, you have my command to declare that our Frater (Soror) has been duly admitted to the 1=10 Grade of Zelator.*

(Kerux comes to the Northwest of Hierophant, faces West, and raises wand.)

Kerux: *In the Name of Adonai Melekh, and by command of the Very Honored Hierophant, hear ye all that I proclaim that Frater (Soror) _____ has been duly admitted to the 1=10 Grade of Zelator, and that he/she has obtained the mystic title of Periclinus (Pericline) de Faustis and the symbol of Aretz.*

(Kerux returns to place by East, saluting, and by South and West.)

Hierophant: *In the Zelator Grade, the symbolism of the tenth Sephirah Malkuth is especially shown, as well as the tenth Path of the Sepher Yetzirah. Among other Mystic Titles, Malkuth is called SHAAR, the Gate, which has the same number as the Great Name ADONAI written in full: Aleph, Daleth, Nun, Yod, which is also called "Gate of Death," "The Gate of Tears," and "The Gate of Justice," "The Gate of Prayer," and "The Gate of the Daughter of the Mighty Ones." It is also called "The Gate of the Garden of Eden" and "The Inferior Mother," and in Christian symbolism is connected with the Three Holy Women at the foot of the cross. The tenth path of the Sepher Yetzirah, which answereth to Malkuth, is called "The Resplendent Intelligence," because it exalts above every head and sitteth upon the Throne of Binah. It illuminateth the Splendor of all the Lights (the Zohar ME-OUROTH) and causeth the current of the Divine Influx to descend from the Prince of Countenances, the great archangel, Metatron.*

*Frater (Soror) _____, before you can be eligible for advancement, to the next grade of 2=9, you will be required to pass an examination on the following subjects:*

1. *Names and symbols of the Three Principles.*

2. *Metals attributed to the Seven Planets.*

3. *The meaning of the special alchemical terms: Sun, Moon, King, etc.*

4. *Names and meanings of the 12 astrological houses.*

5. *Names and meanings of the planetary aspects.*

6. *Names and meanings of the Querent and Quesited.*

7. *The four great classes of astrology.*

8. *The arrangement of the Tree of Life.*

9. *The names of the Four Orders of the Elements.*

10. *The Three Pillars of the Tree of Life.*

11. *The names and forms of the Kerubim.*

12. *Meanings of the Laver, Altar, and Qlippoth.*

13. *The Names of the Ten Houses of Assiah.*

14. *Names of the Four Worlds of the Qabalists.*

15. *Names of the 22 trumps and four suits.*

*A manuscript on these will be supplied to you. When you are well satisfied that you are well informed on these, notify the Officer in Charge.*

## *Closing*

Hierophant: *Fraters and Sorores, assist me to close this temple in the 1=10 Grade of Zelator.*

(All rise.)

Hierophant: *Frater (Soror) Kerux, see that the temple is properly guarded.*

(Kerux knocks on inner side of door. Sentinel returns knock.)

Kerux: *Very Honored Hierophant, the Temple is properly guarded.*

Hierophant: *Let us adore the Lord and King of the Earth.*

(All face East.)

Hierophant: *ADONAI ha-ARETZ, ADONAI MELEKH, Blessed be Thy name unto the countless ages. AMEN.*

(Hierophant gives signs. All give sign and face as usual. Hierophant leaves his/her throne and passes to the North, standing before the Tablet of the North. Hiereus stands on the right of the Hierophant, Hegemon on left hand, Kerux behind Hierophant, Stolistes behind Hegemon, Dadouchos behind Hierophant. Other members behind officers, in alternating lines of sexes where possible.)

Hierophant: *Let us rehearse the prayer of the Earth Spirits.*

    *O, Invisible King, Who, taking the Earth for Foundation, didst hallow its depths to fill them with Thy Almighty Power. Whose Name shaketh the Arches of the World, Thou who causest the Seven Metals to flow in the veins of the rocks, King of the Seven Lights, Rewarder of the subterranean workers, lead us into desirable Air and into the Realm of Splendor. We watch and we labor unceasingly. We seek and we hope, by the 12 Stones of the Holy City, by the buried Talismans, by the Axis of the Loadstone, which passes through the center of the Earth—O Lord, O Lord, O*

*Lord! Have pity upon those who suffer. Expand our hearts, unbind and upraise our minds, enlarge our natures. O Stability and Motion! O Master who never dost withhold the wages of Thy Workmen! O Silver Whiteness—O Golden Splendor! O Crown of Living and harmonious Diamond! Thou who wearest the heavens on Thy Finger like a ring of Sapphire! Thou who hidest beneath the earth in the Kingdom of Gems, the marvelous Seed of the Stars! Live, reign, and be Thou Eternal Dispenser of the treasures whereof thou hast made us the Wardens.* (Pause)

*Depart ye in peace into your abodes. May the blessing of Adonai be upon you.* (Makes banishing pentagram of Earth.) *Be there peace between us and you, and be ye ready to come when ye are called.*

(All return to places and face as usual.)

Hierophant: *In the name of Adonai Melekh, I declare this temple closed in the Grade of Zelator.*

Hierophant: (Makes one battery of four, three, and three knocks)

Hiereus: (Makes one battery of four, three, and three knocks)

Hegemon: (Makes one battery of four, three, and three knocks)

(Candidate is led out by Hegemon.)

# Part 2

# The Commentary

# The 1=10 Earth Grade
# of Zelator

The Zelator Grade of the Golden Dawn relates to the element of Earth and the kabbalistic Sephirah of Malkuth. It is the second of the Golden Dawn initiations, the first being the grade of Neophyte. (See *Z-5: Secret Teachings of the Golden Dawn—Book I: The Neophyte Ritual 0=0* by Pat Zalewski, Llewellyn, 1991, for a full commentary on the Neophyte Ritual.) The state produced by the 0=0 Ritual has been described by some occult authors as being similar to alchemical dissolution. The effect of this first ceremony is vital to the ensuing elemental grades. The 1-10 grade lays the ground for further auric manipulations that the candidate must go through.

The Zelator Grade is more than just an introduction to the ray or power of the Element of Earth. It is a means by which many things analogous to Earth in nature are introduced to the advancing Neophyte. This is done on a level that the candidate would not have recognized before the initiation, due to the subjective influence of the Order itself. The candidate undergoes changes, or transmutations, within his or her psychological makeup after exposure to the auric manipulations of the ritual. This can manifest during, or after, the initiatory process.

In layman's terms, the Earth Grade of Zelator is said to "ground" the student's aura by giving him or her a sense of proportion. This will manifest itself on both the etheric levels of the body and on a day-to-day basis.

Some Golden Dawn people consider the elemental grades to be unimportant. They have substituted ceremonies such as the "Opening by Watchtower" instead of going through the elemental grades. Jack Taylor, however, was very adamant that every student should go through the elemental grades. He felt the grades exerted a positive influence on many levels of the student's life.

Using the Opening by Watchtower as a replacement for the elemental grades can cause unexpected problems. When doing this type of ceremony as an initiation, the aura becomes impregnated with one or more of the Elements. The aura of a novice is not given adequate time to adjust to the vibrational rate. Mass confusion can develop because the individual Elements do not have a chance to strengthen and balance each other in correct sequence. The subtle stops and prompts within the Zelator Ritual do not appear in the Watchtower ceremony, and these have a very real place in the Earth Ritual.

The Zelator Grade is the first of the four main filtration processes of the Outer Order of the Golden Dawn. This ceremony is supposed to try to make the student who seeks to join the Order as a means of escape from reality face up to his or her obligations in the Outer World rather than retreat from them. Before any firm development can be undertaken, life must be faced head on; otherwise, these problems will manifest repeatedly when the student goes on to the next levels. If the Zelator Ritual has been performed correctly, then many of those who attain this level as a form of escapism drop out due to the influence of this ceremony. Also, the influence of it will sometimes spill over into the other grade levels—if the student has had insufficient time for this process to manifest itself.

For those people who are earthly by nature, this ceremony will reinforce their strengths without hindering their progress into the next level. There are some who have an earthly nature and a narrow outlook. This grade is designed to widen their field of vision and to show them the practical aspects of their natures. It is done without undue constriction of their intellectual pursuits, by committing themselves to the ideals set by the Order's framework.

The Zelator Grade is also directly related to the *Guph,* or physical body, of the aspirant. When the candidate goes through the ritual, the etheric energies impregnate the aura. This is done to strengthen the body for the trials and tribulations it will undergo as the pressure of the Order's teachings and magnetic manipulations start to take their toll. By this, we do not mean that the ritual will cause ill health. Rather, like homeopathy and natural systems of healing, it may cause dormant illnesses to come to the surface. One of the bodily systems on which this level seems to work best is the alimentary system, the function of which is to expel waste products and poisons from the body. Any dormant illness revealed by the ritual should be confronted and hopefully healed before further advancement through the grades.

In the Golden Dawn paper, "The Microcosm—Man," a very technical description is given of the actions of the kabbalistic soul as applied to the lowest Sephirah, Malkuth. This description is worth repeating, because it shows in detail some of the things the candidate will experience:

> From Malkuth is formed the whole of the physical body under the command and presidency of the Nephesch. The Nephesch is the subtle body of refined astral Light upon which, as on an invisible pattern, the physical body is extended. The physical body is permeated throughout by the rays of the Ruach, of which it is the material completion., The Nephesch shineth through the Material body and formeth the Magical Mirror or Sphere of Sensation. This Magical Mirror or Sphere of Sensation is an imitation or copy of the Sphere of the Universe. The space between the physical body and the

boundary of the sphere of Sensation is occupied by the ether
of the astral world; that is to say, the container or recipient of
the Astral rays of the Microcosm.

The Nephesch is divided into its seven Palaces, combining
the Sephirotic influences in their most material forms. That
is, the world of passions dominated by the Ruach, or by the
world which is beyond. That is, its Sephiroth are passionate,
expressing a passionate dominion. Thus, its three Supernal
Sephiroth, Kether, Chokmah and Binah, are united in a sense
of feeling and comprehending impressions. Its Chesed is
expressed by laxity of action. Its Geburah by violence of
action. Its Tiphareth is expressed by more or less sensual contemplation of beauty, and love of vital sensation. Its Hod and
Netzach, by physical well-being and health. Its Yesod, by
physical desires and gratifications. Its Malkuth by absolute
increase and domination of matter in the material body.

The Nephesch is the real, the actual body, of which the
material body is only the result through the action of Ruach,
which by the aid of the Nephesch, formeth the material body
by the rays of Ruach, which do not ordinarily proceed beyond
the limits of the physical body. That is to say, in the ordinary
man the rays of Ruach rarely penetrate into the sphere of
Sensation.

Shining through infinite worlds, and darting its rays
through the confines of space, in this Sphere of Sensation is a
faculty placed even as a light is placed within a lantern. This
is a certain sense placed in an aperture of the upper part of
the Ruach wherein act the rays from Chokmah and Binah
which govern the reason—*Daath*. This faculty can be thrown
downwards into the Ruach, and thence can radiate into the
Nephesch. It consists of seven manifestations answering to
the Hexagram, and is like the Soul of the Microprosopus or
the Elohim of the human Tetragrammaton. Therefore in the
head, which is its natural and chief seat, are formed the seven
apertures of the head. This is the Spiritual Consciousness as
distinct from the human consciousness. It is manifested in 7
as just said or in 8 if *Daath* be included. The Father is the
Sun (Chokmah). The Mother is the Moon (Binah). The Wind
beareth it in his bosom (Ruach). Its Nurse is the Earth (Nephesch). The power is manifested when it can be vibrated
through the Earth.

## *Of the Temple in Reference to the Sephiroth*

### *First Part*

The Temple as arranged in the first part of the 1=10 Grade of Zelator (see diagram on next page) shows the Tree of Life in Malkuth, a complete Tree of Assiah. The three paths of *Shin, Tau,* and *Qoph,* as illustrated by Hebrew letters above the dais, show the connection to Malkuth from the greater Tree. Kether is shown for the first time in the Outer Order rituals, and it relates to Kether of Assiah, the Higher Self. This is seen by the candidate, in his or her limited comprehension. Kether must be attained and linked to the physical body at the eastern part of the Altar, and under the guardianship of Sandalphon. The Stations relating to the Tree are as follows:

| Officers on the Dais | Station of the Tree | God-form |
|---|---|---|
| Cancellarius | Ain Soph Aur | Thoth |
| Praemonstrator | Ain Soph | Isis |
| Imperator | Ain | Nephthys |
| Hierophant | Kether | Osiris |

I have amended the original Whare Ra ritual to include these four officers.*

The elemental king is also the main coordinator for the tablet.

---

*It has been assumed that these officers do not appear in the elemental grade rituals, but in fact they can. In the old Golden Dawn, the placing of these officers was optional. In the Stella Matutina, these officers were generally included, on the dais, or else their places were taken by the Wardens of the Temple. If they are not present, the Hierophant has to take the responsibility of performing all their functions. This is almost impossible, as the Stella Matutina found out in later years. Though their positions were generally not marked on the temple diagrams for the 1=10 ritual, it was always understood that they would be present. It is in areas like this that the experience of members of the Stella Matutina, in working the rituals, discovered the weak areas of early Golden Dawn ritual and compensated for them. You will note that a complete Tree of Life is on the floor, while the Supernals are duplicated on the dais. The Chiefs or Wardens on the dais reflect the power of the Tree on the floor. If only the Hierophant is used, then he will do similar work, but it will be directly through Kether.

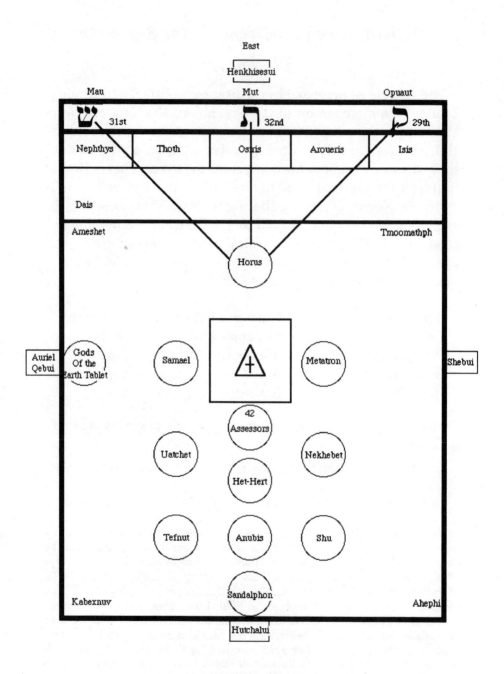

*Tree of Life in Temple*
*(Zelator Ceremony—First Part)*

*1=10 Temple Setup, Part I, View from East*

*Beginning of Part I*

*Invocation Before Earth Tablet*

*Circumambulation*

*Candidate Before Path of Evil*

*Candidate Before Path of Good*

*Candidate Between Path of Good and Evil*

*1=10 Temple Setup, Part II*

He directs what forces go where. During the ceremony, through the temple officers, the elemental king enters the etheric aura of the candidate through the chakra centers. His energies are linked to the diversification factor. He raises the vibrational pitch of the candidate's aura so that it corresponds to the elemental plane related to the Earth element.

The three sets of knocks, totalling 10 in each set, relate to the number of the Sephirah Malkuth. Here the Sephirah is invoked, whereas previously the Earth Element was invoked. This is a good example of the multifaceted principle of Golden Dawn ritual.

## *God-Forms of the 1=10 Grade*

Behind the stations of the Chiefs are the god-forms of the Three Paths.

**Mau**—Mau stands in front of the letter *Shin* and above the Banner of the West. This position curtails the energy of Mau, preventing it from disrupting the ceremony. She has the head of a cat, in green, with twin red feathers above a yellow solar disk. She wears a red robe. Her arm bands are red, as are the ankh and lotus wand which she holds. Mau is shown on page 34.

**Mut**—This god-form stands in front of the letter *Tau* and directly above the throne of the Hierophant. She wears a black vulture's crown with the red and white crown of the North above it. Her nemyss is black-and-white striped. Her dress is black, and her skin is white. Her lotus wand is red and entwined with a green serpent. Mut is shown on page 35.

**Opaut**—This god-form stands in front of the letter *Qoph*. The wolf's head is predominantly crimson with a green waist cloth, armbands, eyes, and ankh. His skin is a light translucent green. He holds a red ankh and lotus wand. Opaut is shown on page 36.

**Isis**—The station of Isis is on the place of the Praemonstrator on the dais. She has a blue headdress on which the emblem of the throne is mounted. Her nemyss is of blue and orange stripes. Her skin is golden yellow and her lower dress is blue with orange straps—the same color as her armbands. She holds

*Mau*

*Mut*

*Opaut*

*Isis*

a green lotus and a red ankh. Isis is shown on page 37.

**Nephthys**—This god-form is on the station of the Imperator. She has a lunar-shaped crown over her black vulture headdress. Her nemyss is black-and-white striped with a necklace of the same color. Her skirt is black with white straps. Her armbands are black-and-white striped. She holds a green lotus and red ankh. Her skin is golden yellow. Nephthys is shown on page 39.

**Thoth**—This God-Form is on the station of the Cancellarius. The color of his ibis head is yellow and mauve. His skin is yellow, while his waistcloth and armbands are mauve. In his left hand he holds a white feather and in the right a white scroll. Thoth is shown on page 40.

**Osiris**—This god-form is on the station of the Hierophant. He wears a white conical cap with the blue feathers of Maat on each side. His skin is green, and he has a black beard. His body wrap is white, his necklace made up of the elemental colors. He holds a red scourge and a red ankh. Osiris is shown on page 41.

**Aroueris**—This god-form sits on the throne of the Past Hierophant. His cap is yellow with a mauve surround and blue feather. His skin is green, and he has a yellow waistcloth and armbands. He hold a blue wand and ankh. Aroueris is shown on page 42.

**Horus**—Horus retains the same position he had in the Neophyte grade, East of the Altar. His face and body are translucent emerald green. He has blue eyes. A curl of blue hair, denoting youth, comes round his face on the right side. He wears the red-and-white double crown. His collar and waist cloth are yellow and blue. His lion's-tail girdle is mauve. His lotus has leaves alternately blue and yellow. Horus is shown on page 43.

**Nekebit**—Nekebit is a figure of light, translucent green with green eyes. Her headdress is shaped like that of Osiris, mainly white with two plumes of gold. Her dress is red with dark green bands. Her staff is black and entwined with a gold Uraeus symbol entwined around it. The collar around her neck is gold, red, and dark blue. She is in the station of the White Pillar. Nekebit is shown on page 44.

*Nephthys*

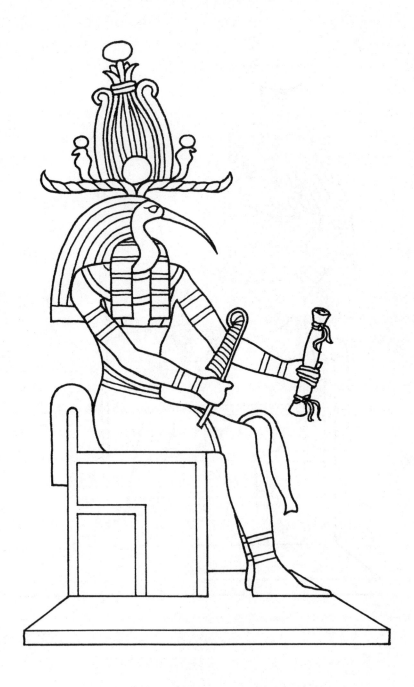

*Thoth*

*Osiris*

*Aroueris*

*Horus*

*Nekebit*

**Uatchet**—This god-form has skin of translucent gold; she wears the black crown of the North with a green feather. Her eyes are black, and her dress is violet with gold bands. She has a black staff with a lotus at the end, which is entwined with a green serpent. Uatchet is shown on page 46.

**Het-Hert**—This Goddess stands at the Western entrance to the Immeasurable Region. She wears green and purple peacock feathers emitting from her pillared crown. Her skin is blackish red; her nemyss is green and red—the same as her collar. Her dress is dark green. She has dark eyes and carries a red ankh and black wand. Het-Hert (or Hathor) is shown on page 47

**Kerub of Air: Henkhisesui**—This Kerub is formed on the farthest eastern boundary. She has the face of a young girl with translucent gold skin and a mauve dress. Her large, spreading wings are a mauve mixture with flashes of golden yellow. Henkhisesui is shown on page 48.

**Kerub of Fire: Shebui**—This Kerub is formed on the farthest reaches of the southern boundary. He has the red head of a lion, large red wings that flash with emerald, and a green tunic. His skin is translucent red. Shebui is shown on page 49.

**Kerub of Water: Hutchaiui**—He has the face of an eagle, and is light blue in coloring. His large spreading wings are blue with flashes of orange. He wears an orange tunic. Hutchaiui is shown on page 50.

**Kerub of Earth: Qebui**—He has the face and form of a bull. He has heavy, darkening wings, of black, green, red, and white. Qebui is shown on page 51.

**Ameshet**—The man-faced Child of Horus is in the Northeast. He has a blue nemyss banded with red, blue, and black. His face is red; he has a black ceremonial beard. Round the shoulders of his white mummy shape are bands of red, blue, and black, three times repeated. Ameshet is shown on page 52.

**Tmoomathph**—The jackal-faced Child of Horus is in the Southeast. He has a black face with yellow linings to his pointed ears. He wears a blue nemyss with borders of black, yellow, and

*Uatchet*

*Het-Hert*

*Kerub of Air: Henkhisesui*

*Kerub of Fire: Shebui*

*Kerub of Water: Hutchaiui*

*Kerub of Earth: Qebui*

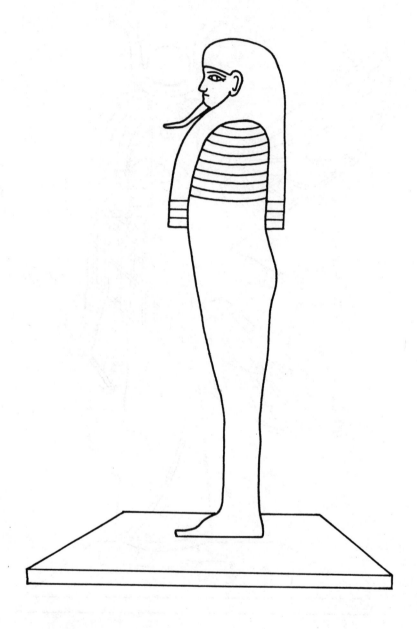

*Ameshet*

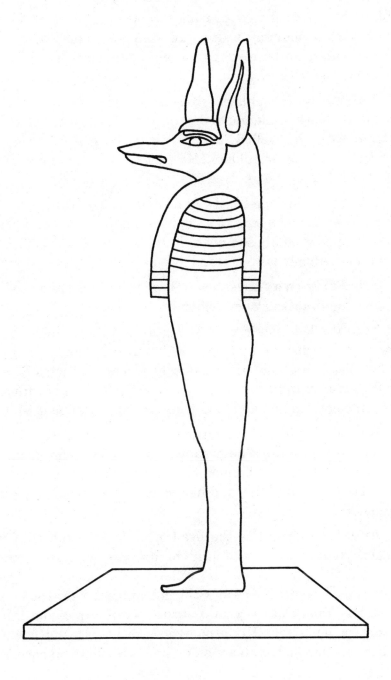

*Tmoomathph*

blue, the same colors appearing threefold at his shoulders. He has a white mummy shape and stands on blue, yellow, and black with a border of green, yellow, and mauve. Tmoomathph is shown on page 53.

**Kabexnuv**—This hawk-faced Child of Horus is in the Northwest. He has a black and tawny face and a nemyss of black bordered with red, yellow, and black. The same colors appear threefold at his shoulders. He has a white mummy shape. Kabexnuv is shown on page 55.

**Ahephi**—This ape-faced Child of Horus is in the Southwest. He has a blue nemyss with red, blue, and yellow bands, These colors appear on his shoulders in the same order. His face is a red color. Ahephi is shown on page 56.

**The Forty-two Assessors**—These god-forms are placed just above the Immeasurable Region.

**Tefnut**—This god-form is in the place of the Dadouchos. She has a green disk and two gold serpents surmounting a golden lion's head. Her body is translucent yellow; his dress is green with a mauve collar and armbands. She holds a staff with a lily mounted on top and an ankh. Tefnut is shown on page 57.

**Shu**—This god-form is in the place of Stolistes. He is blue in color with an orange nemyss and translucent blue skin. His orange clothing is trimmed with gold. The plume from his headdress is dark blue, and he has blue eyes. Shu is shown on page 58.

**Anubis**—Anubis has the head of a black jackal, with very alert, pointed ears—well pricked up. His nemyss is purple banded with white. He wears a collar of yellow and purple bands. His tunic is yellow, flecked with tufts of black hair. His body is red. His waist cloth is yellow striped with purple, and from it hangs a lion's tail. His ornaments are purple and gold; his phoenix wand and ankh are blue. Anubis is shown on page 59.

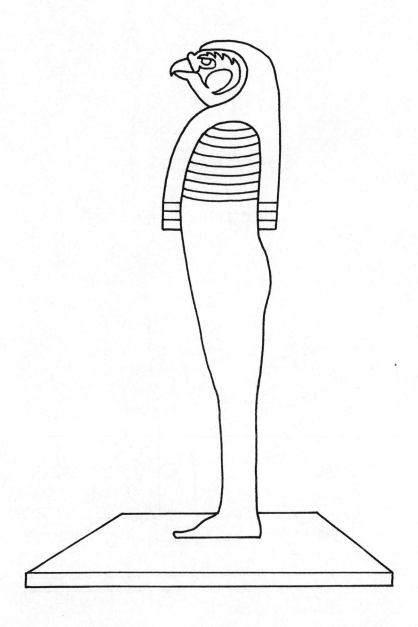

*Kabexnuv*

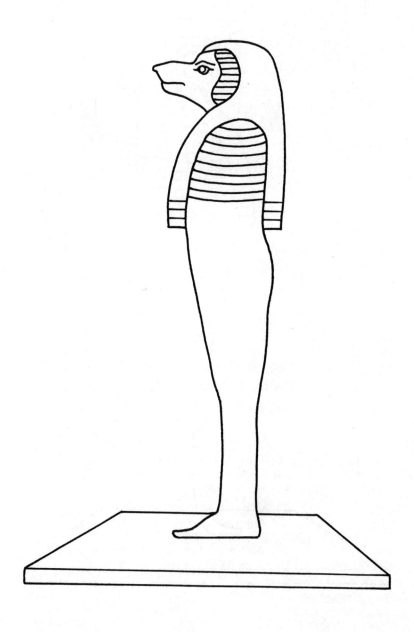

*Ahephi*

*Tefnut*

*Shu*

*Anubis*

## Symbolism of the Temple

The three Hebrew letters that hang above the dais represent the untrodden paths of the candidate. They make up the Hebrew word *qesheth,* a bow. This is said to reflect the rainbow symbol over the dais. The rainbow symbolized by these letters is, by analogy, a bridge between man's higher and lower natures. These letters, being placed above the Chiefs, signify the power of the Second Order manifesting in the First or Outer Order. This represents Higher Knowledge given to those who seek it.

The Altar symbolism shows a cross within a triangle, which shows spirit in matter (a reflection of the topic as discussed in the previous paragraph)—a symbol also for mankind. This is also a symbol of both rejection and knowledge attained. The inference of this symbol is that knowledge can be attained—if the cause of a person's ignorance can be discovered through the teachings of the Order. The symbolism on the Altar is the same as that on the Banner of the West, which is explained in the Zelator Grade: the white triangle refers to the three paths connecting Malkuth with the other Sephiroth, while the red cross is the Hidden Knowledge of the divine name which is to be obtained through their aid. "The cross and triangle together represent Life and Light."

Within the Golden Dawn cipher manuscripts, the red cross is also referred to as the Cross of the Kerubim. This is because of the placing of the Kerubim at the cardinal points, forming a cross. The red cross becomes a cross in the microcosm because of this fact. The red lamp, situated on the Altar, shows the Hidden Knowledge. Its position at the apex of the white triangle shows that this must be attained before the red cross can enter the triangle of Spirit. It becomes the symbolic goal of the candidate.

The symbolism of the Flaming Sword, placed on the western side of the Altar, relates to the paths of both ascent and descent: descent of the divine knowledge into mankind, represented by the candidate, and mankind's aspirations to climb the "Path of Higher Learning" through *kavanah*—devotion. The Black and White Pillars represent the stations of Chesed and Geburah.

*Banner of the West*

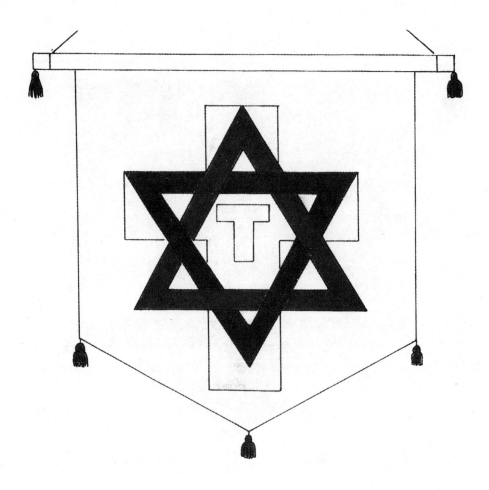

*Banner of the East*

Placed in the position below the Altar, they create the void between light and darkness called, "the Immeasurable Region," which the Higher Self of the candidate must advance through.

The unveiled Enochian Tablet in the North represents the forces of the Earth element and the hierarchies that the candidate must be exposed to during the ritual. These forces are the ones that control the Earth element. The salt, on the side of the Altar directly in front of the Tablet, shows the tangible form that the Tablet represents. The Earth Tablet is the only one of the four present that is unveiled. The others are covered with cloths that have the colors of their respective elements.

The lamp in front of the Earth Tablet relates to the "Ever Burning Lamps" of the Rosicrucian mysteries, which suggest that, once alight, the lamps were never extinguished until an intruder entered the tomb. In this ceremony, the lamp relates to the ever-present offering to the Earth Element. The following Egyptian invocation was given to me by Taylor to say before the Earth Tablet before the start of the ritual:

> *Souls of Tuat, that he that knoweth their name shall be with them. This Great God will give him fields, the situation of which shall be in the country of Ur-Ness. He shall stand up with the Gods who stand up, and he shall follow after this Great God. He shall trample the eater of the Ass, and after the division of the Unoccupied Land has been made, he shall eat bread in the Boat of the Earth.*

The Banners of the East and West are both placed on the dais. This time, instead of guarding against the Qlippoth, the Banner of the West prevents the energies of the Paths from entering into the ceremony.

### *Preparation of the Candidate*

1. Obtain an astrological natal chart of the birth time, or approximate birth time, of the candidate.

2. Prepare an electional chart and marry with the natal chart to decide an appropriate date and time for the ritual.

| b | O | a | Z | a | R | o | p | h | a | R | a |
|---|---|---|---|---|---|---|---|---|---|---|---|
| u/v | N | n | a | x | o | P | S | o | n | d | n |
| a | i | g | r | a | n | o | a/o | m | a | g | g |
| o | r | p | m | n | i | n | g | b | e | a | l |
| r | s | O | n | i | z | i | r | l | e | m | u |
| i | z | i | n | r | C | z | i | a | M | h | l |
| M | O | r | d | i | a | l | h | C | t | G | a |
| R/o | C/O | a/c | n/nm | c | h | i/bt | as/a s | o/s | m/o | t/m | |
| A | r | b | i | z | m | i | i/l | l | p | i | z |
| O | P/p | a | n | a | l/B | a | m | S | m | a | T/L |
| d | O | l | o | P/F | l | n | i | a | n | b | a |
| r | x | p | a | o | c | s | i | z | i | x | p |
| a | x | t | i | r | V | a | s | t | r | i | m |

*Earth Tablet (Watchtower of the North)*

3. Once the time has been established, (which is never on the dark side of the Moon's influence), the candidate is to fast 12 hours, taking nothing except water.

4. Before the ceremony, the candidate should bathe in herbs of the Composite family (which are too numerous to list).

5. For meditation purposes, the candidate is given a small handful of rock-salt crystals some 30 minutes before the ceremony. The candidate is to extend his/her aura to link with the nature of the salt. The candidate is then given a yellow square on a card. S/he should meditate on this card for about 15 minutes before the start of the ceremony.

## *Preparation of the Hall*

1. The temple props are put into place by the Dadouchos, about two hours before the ceremony.

2. The Hierophant enters the Hall, once the Dadouchos has left, and performs the Banishing Ritual of the Pentagram with the Sword of the Hiereus (which should be in its correct station).

3. The Hierophant creates the god-forms of the Visible Stations and the Invisible Stations. He also invokes the power of Earth through the Egyptian invocation.

4. Once all this has been completed, the Chiefs on the dais should enter the temple and create their respective god-forms. If they cannot be present, then it is the Hierophant's duty to create these god-forms.

5. The remaining officers should enter the hall (on a cue from the Hierophant).

6. The candle-lighting ceremony begins when all officers are present.

7. When the candles and lamps are lit in the temple, the officers should assume their respective god-forms, previously created by the Hierophant.

# Symbolism of the Opening

The Hiereus knocks to ask permission of the Hierophant to advance the candidate to the elemental grades. This knock is done with the base of the Sword, on the edge of the chair, and becomes a bridge for the first link with the Altar.*

With the opening speech of the Hierophant, he sends forth

---

*The Hiereus, and not the Hierophant, knocks here as a form of petition for the Hierophant to open up the portal to the elemental grades. This is allied to the Hiereus, acting on behalf of the candidate, to ask permission for the elemental grades to be opened up to the seeker of the Light. It is very important that the Hiereus does this. Taylor put it to us this way: "You do not open the door unless someone seeks admission."

The Office of Sentinel is not dropped after the Neophyte ceremony. The original Golden Dawn copies, and those from Whare Ra Temple, clearly state that this officer is present. The Hiereus holds his sword upright for the entire ceremony. It is only transferred to his right hand when standing in front of the Tablet of Earth, with the edge of the sword turned slightly outward. The cutting edge faces outward, so that no negative influence can penetrate the area guarded by the Hiereus. The Hiereus does not put down the sword, but gives the grade sign with his free right hand. No sign is ever given from a seated position.

the ray of light through his Ruach to the Altar, then to the station of Kerux, thus activating directly the Kerux's station and Sphere of Sensation.

After this, the Kerux sees that the entrance of the Temple is properly guarded. The Hiereus, commanded by the Hierophant, tests those present to insure that they are of 1=10 grade, or higher. This testing procedure is not really for the officers working in the ceremony, but for those present in the hall, outside the portal watching the ceremony. All those within the hall have to reply to the signs at the order of the Hiereus. When all these signs are done in unison, towards the East, it activates the Spheres of Sensation/auras of the temple officers with the god-forms on the temple floor.*

The next phase of operation is the consecration of the Temple with Water and Fire. At this point, the command of the Hierophant specifically states that the Temple be consecrated with Water first and Fire second, yet the reverse is done. The Water and Fire purification, used in both the Inner and Outer Orders of the Golden Dawn, relates directly back to nature. Both the Christian and Hermetic viewpoint apply here equally: the dissolution of the body, after death, through water, with the rising of the Spirit as fire. In only two rituals of the Golden Dawn are the Water and Fire consecrations reversed: the 1=10 Ceremony and the Consecration of the Vault. We believe both are in error, a point Regardie agreed with.

The firm rule of thumb given to all those in the Inner Order, was that, when consecrating an inanimate object, use Water and then Fire. When consecrating a person, with Earth, the reverse occurs. This should be the only exception. In the Golden Dawn cipher manuscripts (see *Secret Inner Order Rituals of the Golden Dawn)*, Fire and then Water is the order given for con-

---

*When the officers link or submerge themselves in the god-form of the station that they represent, during the candle-lighting ceremony, they only link to the lower levels of that god-form. The Hierophant, during this first show of signs, completes this by linking the Supernals of the Sphere of Sensation, through the nemysses of the temple officers. After this, the only other link with the god-forms is to the element of Earth.

secrating the candidate. Mathers suggested that the consecration of the Temple follow the same pattern.

There is a good reason in the 1=10 for the candidate to be purified with Fire first. He or she has just completed the 0=0 grade and is at a level where Fire and salt (representing the Earth Element) are analogous to each other. The next alchemical step is a dissolution to water again. Overall, the author(s) of the Golden Dawn ciphers had a marvelous understanding of nature by injecting the reversal principle.*

However, no matter which way it is viewed, the initial consecration of the Temple should be by Water and then by Fire, with the reverse occurring later in the ceremony for the candidate. In the New Zealand order, we have amended our ritual papers so that the Stolistes purifies first.

Also note that the purification by Water is done from the Pillars, in the order of the ascent of the Lightning Flash, which fits in with the overall picture. This aspect is destroyed when Fire is utilized as the first consecration.

The actual consecration is done slightly above the Stations of the Pillars in order to help clear a path to the Ruach of the ceremony. This helps clear the way for the Breath of Life to be received, not only from the East, but also from the North of the Temple as well.

With the speech of the Hierophant, "Let the Element of this Grade be named that it may be awakened in the spheres of those and in the sphere of the Order," all of the officers present activate the earthly part of their auras, charged in previous rituals by the Enochian Tablets. This is done through visualization of the yellow square that the candidate was asked to meditate on before the ceremony.

Before this is done, the officers do the Adoration to Earth, which gives them their initial connecting link. The kabbalistic

---

*See Jung's *Mysterium Coniunctionis* for a full explanation of the Water/Fire combination and discussion of associated alchemical texts. The section on "Personification of Opposites" and the subsections, "Regeneration of Sea Water" and "The Interpretation and Meaning of Salt," are of particular interest, as they present the Christian, Pagan, and Hermetic viewpoints.

cross unites both the macrocosm and the microcosm of the Earth element, which is necessary before linking to the Tablets because they also have a dual link to Earth.

The movement by the Hierophant, when making the cross with the scepter, is directed slightly upward to the sign of Tau hanging above the dais. All those present have previously travelled this path during their own initiations into the Earth element. The following is from an unpublished Golden Dawn document by Mathers, dated 1897:

> Let the Officers formulate the Yellow Cube of Earth around them and let their Sphere of Sensation filleth with every expression of Earth so that their very being is enflamed with Salt of the Earth when the Hierophant linketh with Tau through Cross and Circle . . .

The Hierophant then goes clockwise to the North and places himself in a position approximately six feet in front of the Earth Tablet with the other officers forming behind him (see figure on next page).

What occurs here is almost a complete pivot of the temple, with the Kerux remaining at his original station to maintain the stream of Light directed by the Hierophant earlier. This helps stabilize the Altar for its fusion with the direct energy from the Earth Tablet.*

The speech by the Hierophant in front of the Tablet is a method whereby the power of the Earth is formulated like that of human beings (even in the macrocosm) so that it is subjected to the same rules as all living creatures, whether spiritual or otherwise, and can be controlled by the Temple officers (Gen. I:26-27).

In other words, the Hierophant formulates an archetypal fig-

---

*In the "Introduction to the Elemental Grades," in Israel Regardie's *The Golden Dawn* (Llewellyn, 6th ed., 1989), it states that the officers form a hexagram in front of the Tablets. Since the Kerux remains in his station, this is not quite the case. The Altar remains as the lowest portion of the hexagram and, from this configuration, becomes the recipient of the energy about to be drawn from the Tablets.

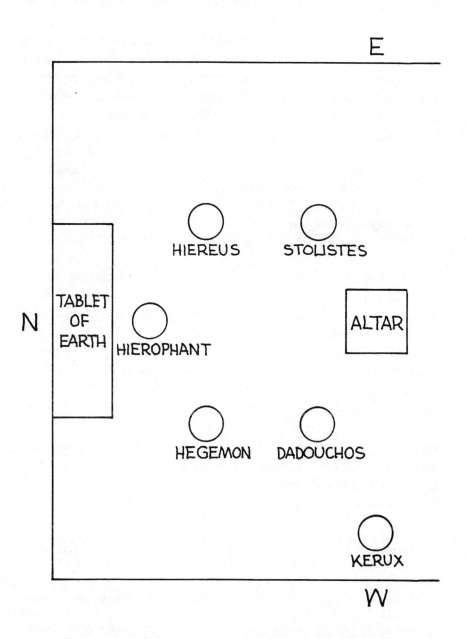

*Hierophant and Officers Before Earth Tablet*

ure of the archangel Auriel when invoking with Spirit. When
directly invoking with the Earth pentagram, this figure can be
reduced in size.*

The Hierophant takes the sword of the Hiereus. He formulates
the Sign of the Ox , which represents the Kerub of Earth, who is
also invoked in turn. At this juncture, the outermost reaches of
the element have been brought under control. An unpublished
Golden Dawn paper by Mathers on the subject says:

> . . . Create the Blue Circle in the astral then project it through
> the Tablet to the very quarter where the Great Arch-angel
> Auriel standeth. The Pentagrams of Spirit and Earth shall blin-
> deth him with their Brilliance while the force of the Sword will
> commandeth the Ox, the Great Kerub of Earth who standeth
> before Auriel though he be somewhat smaller in stature.

This is part of the technique taught in the training of the
Hierophant. The Hierophant's scepter acts as a type of long-
range blasting rod, used to open, close, and connect to the
sword. It is used for invocation and evocation.†

In this elemental ceremony, the invoking pentagram reacts
through the tablets, and not at them, as this is its direction. The
use of the ox is one example where the Kerub, and not the Tablet,
is invoked. In the Opening by Watchtower, one only invokes the
Tablet when the Three Holy Names applicable to the Tablet are
called as part of making the invoking pentagram. During this
opening, the invoking wand is not the Hierophant's Scepter, but
the cross, chain, cup, and dagger, which are analogous to the ele-

---

*Within the old Golden Dawn, and later in the Stella Matutina, both
active and passive pentagrams were drawn before the actual invoking elemental pentagram. It is now considered common practice to do either the
active or passive pentagram relating to the element concerned rather than the
actual elemental invoking pentagram.

†At this point, we would refer the reader to *Part I: The Neophyte Ritual
0=0,* which described the misuse of the Hierophant's scepter as an invoking
instrument during the Opening by Watchtower, and yet it appears to be doing
the same thing in the elemental ceremonies, although the Z.1 document
warns against such action. This has caused a great deal of confusion.

mental weapons and are Second Order instruments. Book I of the Z-5 series, *The Neophyte Ritual 0=0,* explains further use of the Hierophant's scepter. All further actions in front of the Tablet are passive gestures, such as the cross, to establish an empathy with the ceremony only—not to take the full brunt of its power and inject them into the candidate.

Once the Hegemon's wand is used to make the cross in front of the Tablet, it brings the energy of the Tablet into life through the Earth element. This is done through the Kerub of Earth, by the power of Adonai. With the Cup of Stolistes, a cross is drawn in the air in front of the Tablet. With the most passive weapon available, an empathy is created with the Three Holy Names of EMOR DIAL HCTGA. The Three Holy Names are the keys to tapping the power of the Earth Tablet.*

The Hierophant makes a cross with the censer and calls forth the name of the elemental king, IC ZOD HE CHAL. Under normal circumstances, these names would automatically be awakened by the calling of the Three Holy Names, but when called on directly by the Hierophant, it is done for a specific purpose—to direct the power of the Tablet.

In consecrations and grading ceremonies, the ray of the elemental king is the first to impregnate the aura of the respective

---

*The oral teachings, from Whare Ra Temple state that each of the Three Holy Names represents an astrological house. During the ceremony, these names affect the second to fourth houses and directly affect the life of the candidate in the three areas, which are as follows:

EMOR: Second House. Affects the possessions of the candidate and is meant to guide and arm him with the necessary values of this life. Taylor called this the "grounding" or "earthing" of the candidate, which instills a balance, helping him to cope with day-to-day activities.

DIAL: Third House. This affects the communicative ability of the candidate and helps him to strengthen the bond between friends and family, as well as helping him to face problems on this level of existence.

HCTGA: Fourth House. Here, the inherited tendencies of the candidate are being helped and directed towards a common good.

The fundamental philosophy behind this is that, as the candidate goes through the four elemental grades, he goes through the 12 astrological houses. Each one of these is strengthened in turn, thus helping the candidate function on the level of mind, body, and spirit.

object. The Hierophant creates a vital etheric link by merging his aura with that of the Tablet, and then with the object in question, during pertinent parts of the ceremony. When this force is withdrawn at the close of the ceremony the vibration, in empathy, continues apart from the etheric link. The elemental king is also the main coordinator for the Tablet, and directs which forces go where.

During the ceremony, through the temple officers, the elemental king enters the etheric aura of the candidate through the chakra centers. His energies are linked to the diversification factor. He raises the vibrational pitch of the candidate's aura so that it corresponds to the elemental plane related to the Earth element.

## *Advancement: First Part*

The Hierophant announces that a dispensation has been given to admit the candidate and orders the Hegemon to give the customary alarm.*

The Hegemon goes clockwise to the antechamber, where the candidate is blindfolded and given the Cubical Cross. The Hegemon instructs the candidate in the correct knocks to gain entrance to the hall. The Kerux holds the door ajar and by doing so creates a gap in the portal of the ceremony, which in the 1=10 should extend to the door of the antechamber. With the door open, the portal is kept slightly open. The Hegemon and Sentinel form a triangle with the Kerux.

The figure on the following page shows the temporary break or gap in the portal, which is balanced on the outside by the Hegemon and Sentinel. If a Sentinel is not present, the Hegemon con-

---

*This is taken from Psalm 127 and shows yet another layer of Golden Dawn ritual training—the magical use of the biblical Psalms. Although scholars have written extensively on this subject, we would refer the reader to a work that Mathers was familiar with, and often used. This is *The Magical Use of the Psalms,* which was published originally in 1788. There were a number of notations (with Mathers' initials) that referred to the magical uses of the Psalms on a Golden Dawn master copy of the 1=10 Ritual. This particular Psalm was said to protect a newborn child immediately after birth. The Golden Dawn modified this to protect the candidate after entrance to the hall.

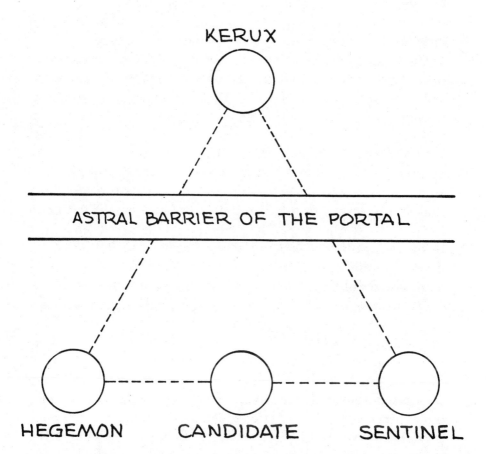

*A Temporary Break in the Portal*

trols the opening and closing of the portal. The symbology of the Kerux dimming the lights is twofold. First, the candidate enters a new area to him or her, the blackness of the Void. Second, with the symbolic lowering of the lights, the Hierophant lowers the vibrational pitch of the portal and allows the candidate to breech it, while the Kerux and Hegemon hold the vortex together.

The candidate gives the signs, word, grip, etc., of the Neophyte Grade to show that he has passed the previous initiation. The candidate carries the Fylfot Cross in his right hand, and it is taken by the Kerux, who holds it right up until the time when the cross is explained to the candidate. He is then placed between the Pillars. His Higher Self is held in check, not only by the current of the Neophyte, but also by the Goddess Het-Hert, Guardian of the Immeasurable Region. As the candidate kneels, with his right hand on the earth and with his left hand throws salt to the North, he uses the "As is above and so is below" principle. The element he touches with his left hand, the microcosm and the macrocosm of the Earth element in nature, extends not only in the soil, but to the stars as well.

The next phase of the operation is the purification of the candidate by Fire and then by Water.* In the next phase of the operation, the Hierophant describes the fundamental floor of the Temple (one level of it, that is), which is the Tree of Life of Malkuth of Assiah. In doing so, the Immeasurable Region becomes measurable, for the candidate has been provided with a blueprint of the Tree of Life (which he learned in the previous grade). The controlling power on the floor at this time is the god-form of Het-Hert. She has formed a cocoon or astral station around the candidate as a form of protection, and also as a guide. The Kerux, as Anubis, leads the candidate towards the station of Samael, where he is challenged by the Hiereus,

---

*Here, the candidate has achieved the status of salt of Fire. To go on to the next phase, which is a reduction to the watery principle, he is purified with Fire, then with Water. The biblical quotations from Matthew 5:13, "Ye are salt of the earth," and Mark 9:50, "have salt in yourselves and peace with one another . . .," all relate to peace and wisdom being analogous to salt, marking a higher level of understanding.

telling him of the area he cannot enter. Here, the god-form of Het-Hert has saved the candidate from certain oblivion, and now draws him back along the way he came, guided by Anubis.

At the command of the Hierophant, the candidate goes towards the Pathway of Good. The god-form of Metatron, in the form of the Hegemon, dazzles the candidate with his brilliance. Once again, he is protected by Het-Hert, who softens the glare and protects him from the glory of the reflected godhead. Upon returning to the station from which he started, the candidate has learned that there are no shortcuts to the Hidden Knowledge, lest he be blinded by the brightness of what he will find or corrupted by the darkness that could engulf him. This is also the first lesson in patience. Now, therefore, at the command of the Hierophant, he enters the Middle Path. At this point, the candidate is conducted to the foot of the Altar, guided by Anubis in the form of the Kerux.

When the candidate is a foot in front of the Altar, he is barred by the Hiereus and Hegemon, who cross their elemental weapons before the Altar.*

This barring is done by the lower Sephiroth of the Supernals of the Tree of Assiah. When the Hierophant comes forward, he uses the Light from his scepter to unblock the energies of the higher Supernals.

At this juncture, the energies start to change the aura of the candidate, concentrating indirectly on the lower chakra center on the back through the kabbalistic Sephirah of Malkuth around the feet of the candidate. The Hierophant opens up the energies of the Tree. As he comes forward, he assumes the form of Sandalphon, desiring to link with Metatron in Kether. Guided by Sandalphon, the candidate is then shown the drawing at the base of the Altar.†

---

*Both officers turn clockwise to face West, as they generally face East and only turn for specific reasons.

†Genesis 2:24, for the speech of the Hierophant. Although Metatron is associated with Chokmah, this is very much the level of reflected glory, toned down, so that the candidate is able to grasp his energies. Metatron inhabits Kether, but works through Chokmah, though, at this point, the energies are now directed from Kether due to the efforts of the Hierophant as Sandalphon.

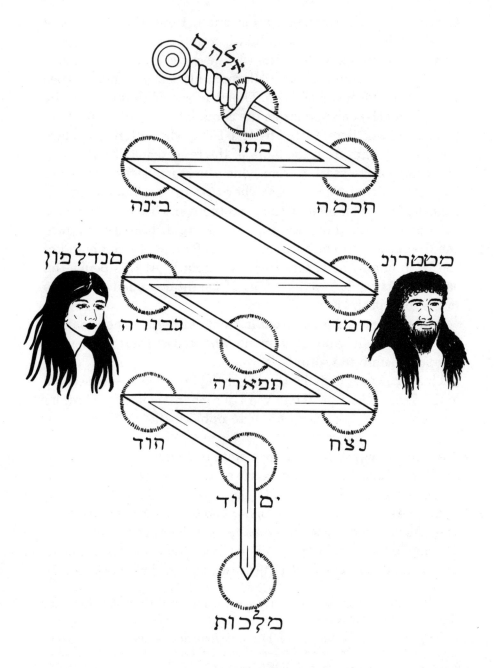

*The Flaming Sword*

The diagram of the Flaming Sword (at left) shows the descent of the energy through the Tree, from Kether to Malkuth. An unpublished Golden Dawn document states: ". . . the Hierophant, as the Great Sandalphon, sheweth his power through the grasp which giveth the power of Metatron to the Neophyte . . ." What Mathers was trying to show here was that the Hierophant should draw the power of Metatron through his scepter, from the Altar, and then directly inject this into the aura of the candidate, through the grip with which he hold the candidate. The Hierophant actually points in the general direction of the Altar—or to be more precise, the top of it—where the interconnecting currents of energy cross. He draws directly from this juncture.*

The candidate is invested with the Step, the Sign, the Word, the Number, and the Password. Of this, the most important is the Sign, which is given by raising the right hand to a 45-degree angle. The higher teachings of this sign relate it to the power of the Earth, for during any astral contact with any entity, this sign may be given as a sign of its Earth nature.†

The Hegemon draws the candidate's attention to the Flaming Sword and explains its symbolism, which the candidate experienced directly at the hands of the Hierophant. The symbolism of the cross in the triangle is in essence much the same as the Flaming Sword principle—Spirit descending into matter.

The general meaning of the Enochian Tablet of Earth is given

---

*This method of energy transference, by touch, is a very old one. Taylor demonstrated this transference to us. He could project energy into an aura eight feet away, without touching, and achieve the same result—but without use of a scepter. To do this, one invokes Metatron, through AHIH. The energy is transferred to the candidate by way of Sandalphon. As the energy goes into the candidate, it manifests itself from the top of the head down, much in the same manner as in the diagram.

†When contacting plant life, one will often find, when requesting that the spirit of the plant reveal its nature, that it will give a series of elemental signs, which are generally a mixture of more than one element. By performing this sign when one invokes the element of Earth during the invoking pentagram ritual, additional force is brought to bear that results in more control for the user. It is also used extensively in alchemical operations. The actual lifting of the hand signifies the raising of the veil to allow the forces of Metatron to mingle with those of Sandalphon in the Tree of Assiah.

and related back to the angel Ave and the biblical Book of Enoch.*

The Fylfot Cross† is handed to the candidate by the Kerux, and is explained as pertaining to the solar system in general, with the Sun, four elements, and 12 signs of the zodiac given. The Kerux then takes the candidate out.

The next gesture, by the Hierophant, is something that was dropped in many Golden Dawn temples, including Whare Ra, except when Jack Taylor was Hierophant. He continued to teach the way of his teacher, who was a protege of Felkin. In order to close the Hall for the first part of the ceremony, without due disruption to the next part, the Hierophant grasps the uppermost grip of the scepter, the Path of Gimel and, with a movement of the cross, temporarily closes the Temple. The wording for this was left up the individual Hierophant, but the gesture and purpose had to be clear. The use of the Gimel part of the scepter effectively cuts off the power from the Supernals of the Tree, as the grip is above Daath. The god-forms and stations will only exist for a short period of time. The initial current of power will still come through, but will be held in abeyance.

------

*The Inner Order H Document, *"Clavicula Tabularum Enochi,"* as it is sometimes called, states:

> Now as to the general significance of the tables, and of the Officers of the Angels, and other remarkable observations, these tables contain all human knowledge; they stretch to the knowledge of Solomon: for out of it springeth Physic, the knowledge, finding, and use of all metals, the virtues of them, the congelations and virtues of stones (they are all of one matter)—the knowledge of all Elemental Creatures amongst us, how many kinds there are, or what they are created. Those that live in the Air, Water, or Earth, by themselves. The property of Fire, which is the secret life of all things:— but more particularly, the knowledge of all mechanical craft whatsoever; the secrets of man, the moving from place to place, as in the country etc. The knitting together of Nature, and of things that may perish; as well as the enjoying and knitting them together, etc.

†The Fylfot Cross, shown on the next page, is a universal symbol, appearing in early American, European, and Oriental cultures. Its two shapes relate to the passive and active principle. The counterclockwise shape of the Golden Dawn version relates to the inward spiral and Goddesses, such as Artemis and Astarte, who are attributed to the Earth and the feminine attributes. The oral teachings of the Golden Dawn relate the Fylfot to the swirling power of the Sephirah Malkuth, that revolves inward so that the energy then goes back up through the Middle Pillar of the Tree to Kether.

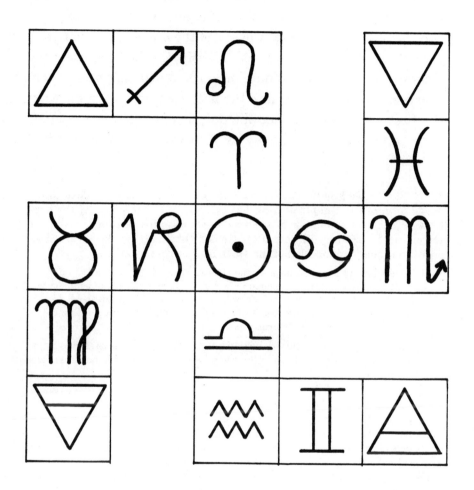

*The Fylfot Cross*

## *Part Two**

When all officers are seated, the Hierophant will, by the Gimel grip of the scepter, open the ceremony in exactly the same way as he closed it at the end of the previous session, with only the wording being altered slightly. He then instructs the Kerux to admit the candidate once the alarm has been given. The position of the entry into the hall is exactly the same as in the first part, though, once the door is open, the Kerux steps back, and the candidate steps forward, with the Sentinel directly behind him.

---

*The Temple ground plan, shown on the following page, relates to the astral form of the Temple of New Jerusalem. Dr. Felkin's copy of the book *Cannon* contains a number of sections which describe certain parts of the Outer and Inner Order Rituals of the Golden Dawn. The particular passage, ascribed to the "Ground Plan of the 1=10, Second Part," states:

> The name of the Tabernacle in the Hebrew (Ex. XXV.9) is MShKN, and yields 1060, one less than one length of a vesica 612 broad, two numbers are found in the names of Apollo and Zeus . . . The number 1060 is also the diagonal of a square whose sides are 749.5, and this square is contained within a rhombus ascribed within Saturn's orbit.

(The figure of the enclosed hexagram for the second part helps show exactly where everyone and everything is placed, and why. This has been previously unpublished.)

Saturn is also ascribed to the element of Earth. The circumference relates to the portal, or edge of the magical aspects of the ceremony. The lines show the main currents of power running through the Temple, while the Hegemon is seated directly in the center of the Temple.

Each officer has charge over one or more items that are removed and replaced with the necessary props for the second part of the ceremony. These generally pertain to his or her role in the ceremony. The officers all move silently and efficiently and in a clockwise manner, and, although the Supernals are sealed by the Hierophant, the Temple is not closed, for it sits in a state of suspended animation, and no loud or sudden movement or unnecessary talk must take place to disrupt the energies.

The Hierophant supervises the Temple transformation, noting that all is in place. A diagram kept hidden in his clothing is advisable, as the "high" from the ceremony tends to make people light-headed, and things can easily be forgotten. It is advisable to keep replacement diagrams and ornamentations, etc., inside the side altars.

*Note:* No one must cross the portal throughout the duration of the ceremony except where explicitly stated in the ritual.

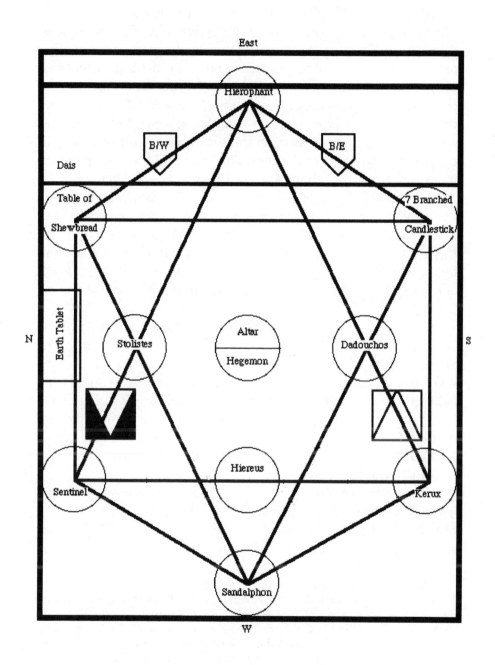

*Temple of Jerusalem Applied to Second Part*

They form another triangle, with the candidate at the apex. The Hierophant tells him where the Symbolic Altar of Sacrifices stood in the Court of the Tabernacle, which relates to the Qlippothic or negative influences which were left behind during the previous purification. Dadouchos purifies the candidate with a cross and three swings of the censer. This forms the symbol of the cross in the triangle (each swing being a point of the triangle) which is also the symbol on the Altar. Here the link is picked up from the first part of the ceremony. The Stolistes also purifies in a similar manner, giving equal balance to the purification rite.

The Hierophant tells the candidate of the symbolism of the Laver of Brass, and its relationship to purification in the Old Testament. The term "Waters of Creation" had its roots in both Egyptian and Hebrew symbolism, for water is the symbol of birth, which in this instance is analogous to the new beginning of the candidate and is to a certain extent a replica of the magical meaning of Psalm 127.

The candidate is taken to the North, where he is barred by the Hiereus. On giving the Grip and Signs of the Neophyte, he advances to a position between the Pillars. Hegemon comes forward to face him, and he is again challenged. This time, he is asked to give the Grip and Signs of the Zelator. Kerux returns to his seat, while Hegemon escorts the candidate to the diagram of the Table of Shewbread (see next page), which represents the 12 zodiac signs, the 12 tribes, the 12 loaves, and the 12 Foundations of the Holy City.*

The pressure of the grip of the Hegemon is increased dramatically while he explains the symbolism of the Table of the Shewbread. This diagram is more than a mere diagram of 12 colored triangles, for it has a station of its own in this part of the ritual.

---

*At this point we are shown an Outer Order version of the diagram. Mathers expanded more fully on this diagram in the Practicus Adeptus Minor Grade, under the heading of "The Knowledge of the Ritual of the 12 Gates in Skrying and Travelling in the Spirit Vision; answering to the Diagram of the table of the Shewbread." As one advanced through the four levels of the 5=6 grades, the Inner Order explanation of this diagram was then made clear. (See *Secret Inner Order Rituals of the Golden Dawn,* page 174. Part of this previously unpublished lecture is included in *Golden Dawn Enochian Magic.*

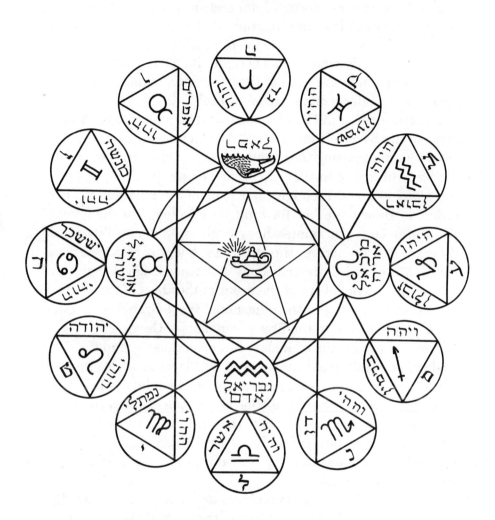

*Table of Shewbread*

(Very few of the Golden Dawn diagrams were colored. At Whare Ra, the Adept would often go back and color the diagrams in the colors of his or her choosing. I am unaware of what the temples in England did.) It is the function of the Hegemon to link the Ruach of the candidate to the flashing tablet of the shewbread, for this is exactly what it has become. Its energy is directed by the Hegemon into the aura of the candidate, to make him more aware of the effects of nature on himself.

The Hegemon and Hiereus conduct the candidate to the diagram of the Seven-Branched Candlestick (shown on next page), where its relationship to the number seven is given. This shows similar influences to that of the preceding diagram, but on a more direct mode. Through the Ruach of the Hiereus, the candidate is shown another flashing set of colors. On the level of the Outer Order, it relates heavily to the planets. When this diagram is presented in the Practicus Adeptus Minor curriculum of Mathers, it is described as "The Knowledge of the Secret Ritual of the symbolism of the order of the Days of the Week of Creation, answering to the diagram of the 7-Branched Candlestick." Its roots are in the first seven days of Genesis.*

From this point, the candidate has been taken the route of the Lightning Flash, from the base of the Tree. It is designed to instill in him a concept of learning. The candidate is led to the West of the Altar where the Hierophant comes forward swinging the censer (in the shape of the cross in the triangle) and gives the speech concerning the Altar of Incense.

The Altar of Malkuth is a physical representation of the spiritual Altar of Incense.

The title of Zelator, or *Pereclinus de Faustis,* is bestowed on the candidate. It is to remind him of the early alchemical theme of the Rosicrucian grades. The Zelator was the stoker for the athanor of the alchemist, the most menial of all tasks with which to begin his apprenticeship in magic. Its vibratory pitch opens up the mysteries of the Earth element for the student.

---

*Refer to *Golden Dawn Enochian Magic* for full Inner Order explanation of diagram.

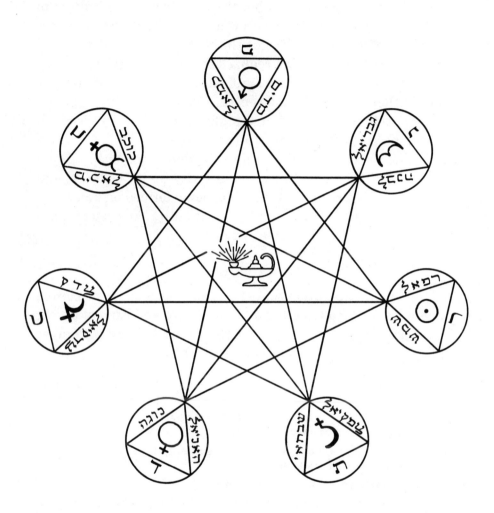

*Seven-Branched Candlestick*

The Zelator is led to a seat in the Northwest by the Kerux, who uses his wand to indicate where he must go. The Kerux institutes the proclamation that the Zelator is now admitted to the mysteries of *Aretz,* the Hebrew name for Earth. The "Thirty-two Paths of Wisdom" calls this the "Path of Resplendent Intelligence." On this path, one realizes that one is in Malkuth. By that virtue, one attains the unification with the luminations from Kether, because of the central Pillar of the Tree. The old saying, "Kether is Malkuth and Malkuth is Kether," very much applies here. The reference to the "Throne of Binah" by the Hierophant is very complex. It must be remembered that Binah is the first separation of feminine polarity from Chokmah, and gives the first stirrings of a new life, being formed on an as-yet-unmanifested level, which relates to an entire Tree before manifesting in a new area of development.*

## *Closing*

After the proclamation that the Temple is about to be closed, all officers face the East and adore the Lord and King of Earth. They form a hexagram in front of the Tablet and say the prayer of the Earth Spirits in front of the Tablet.†

---

*The meanings of some of the titles of Malkuth, as given in the speech of the Hierophant, are as follows:

"Gates of the Shadow of Death"—This shows the karmic pattern of lives one lives through in which one never really dies.

"Gate of Justice"—This shows that everything must be balanced before ascension to the next level of existence.

"Gate of Prayer"—This shows the devotional aspect of life.

"Gate of the Daughter of the Mighty Ones"—This relates to the birth of Earth itself, in terms of planetary relationships.

"Gate of the Garden of Eden"—The entrance way to the state of the Divine is through Earth and human incarnations.)

†This prayer is taken from Levi's *Transcendental Magic,* and, though there are some differences, they appear to be in that of translation from the French, as this book was not translated into English until 1896—some years after the elemental rituals had been written. The gnomes are the elemental spirits of Earth. Their king, Ghob, was said to live in the subterranean areas of the Earth and to have control of all metals.

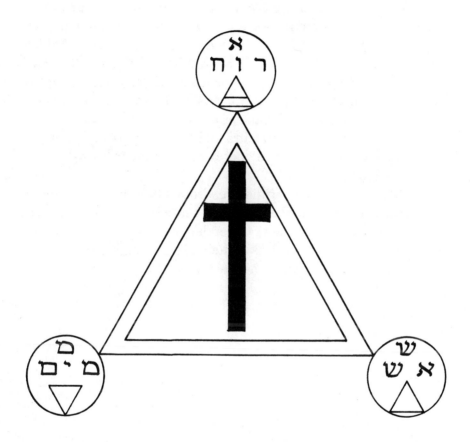

*Altar*

The Banishing Ritual of the Pentagram is done with the Hierophant's scepter, after the command to depart in peace. Again, this is done through the Earth Tablet rather than directly from it. The grade is closed with the 10 knocks of Malkuth by the Hierophant and Hegemon.

Once the prayer to the elements is read out in front of the Tablet, and the elementals are told to depart, the Earth aspect of the ceremony winds down. The elemental king of the Tablet of Earth starts to withdraw his energy from the tablet. The use of the scepter here cuts the power from the ceremony and also defuses the god-forms. The god-forms on the dais dematerialize, followed by those of the Temple officers. By the time those in the Temple leave the hall, their auras will be magnetically charged from the ceremony, but the god-forms around them will have ceased to exist.

The allocution is sometimes read out after the ceremony is finished. If so, all members remain seated until it is finished. This aspect of the ceremony depended on how vocal the Hierophant was feeling, and it was included in the candidate's copy of the ritual to study at his or her leisure.

# Part 3

# Whare Ra Lectures and Addresses

# Lecture on the 1=10 Ceremony for the Zelator Grade Whare Ra Temple

## Introduction

Fraters et Sorors:

In order that we may get our ideas thoroughly into form, and be prepared to consider the symbology of the 1=10 Grade, it might be well just for a moment recall what each of us considers the purpose for which we are all associated together. For unless we have some real earnest purpose behind what we do, and impelling us, these our ceremonies are mere burlesque, and unworthy of the attention of grown men and women.

Now, I think there can be no doubt that for all of us the primary idea is that of self-development in some line or another. It matters not for the present what that line is, but we hope somehow or other to make ourselves nobler, wiser or better men and women than we were when we started. And also we hope to gain a further knowledge of the Inner Secrets of Nature, in that we may know more and be able to use those powers of nature whose existence we are conscious of but whose modes of opera-

tion are hidden from the ordinary brain of man, hidden therefore from the man of materialistic science, and therefore called
ordinary Occult. We wish to search out nature that thereby we
may come more in contact with Nature's GOD.

I think that summarizes the position of all of us, although I
suppose that the aim of every one is to some extent divergent.

Well, now, we believe that in this Order we can obtain a certain amount of help in that great quest. And I think, that all we
who have got so far as to pass through the veil that separates
the Outer from the Inner, can assure you who are still in the
Outer that there is a great deal of help which is given in this
Order. One or two ways which are given you may allow me to
point out.

One is unknown to you and therefore you must take it on
faith, and that is, that one of the Chiefs of the Temple primarily,
and all the members of the Second Order to an appreciable
extent, but in a less degree, do occult-wise bring an influence, a
current of Will, to bear upon all members of the Outer from the
Neophyte Grade up to the Grade of 4=7 which insensibly to
themselves changes their nature, changes their character and
their pose of mind towards the material and Outer Universe.
You are not conscious of this. Only the most developed natural
sensitives can be conscious of it, and only in a very vague and
slight degree. Nevertheless, it does exist, and those of the Second Order who are sufficiently trained to develop their spiritual
and clairvoyant perceptions, can perceive it. They can perceive
the change in you which you yourselves for the time being are
unconscious of until you attain some level and are able to look
back on your previous course. Then you will see how that
change gradually worked in you.

But there is another way in which this Order helps you, and
that is by its Ceremonies, and by the symbolism of these Ceremonies, because as you gradually come to understand the symbolism of grade after grade you will see that they are really, as
it were, algebraic formulae which teach you how to develop
yourselves in the first instance, how to guide, govern and rule
your own body, in order that hereafter, when you have learned

that lesson, you may apply the same formulae precisely to the influencing of the Outer World. First of all you must learn to guide and regulate and govern yourselves and your own bodies. Secondly, you may be allowed to influence material bodies beyond and outside yourselves.

Now, I have spoken, and some of you probably remember it, on the symbolism of the 0=0 Grade, and in that lecture I pointed out that the temple, as arranged for the 0=0 Grade, actually represented in a miniature diagram as it were, the whole of existence, that is to say everything that the Creator has breathed forth into being, and that the *cubical altar* in the centre represented the Material Universe, the Officers representing the various powers by which the Will of the Creator operates upon that Material Universe. And that first teaches you how small in the general scheme of the universal Existence, is what we know as the Material Universe and of the ten squares constituting the Cubical Altar, only one, and that basal square, the square that stands upon, represents the utmost part of the *material Universe* which you can see, handle or hear, or know by the five senses, and that from the position of the Altar, is hidden.

From the time, therefore, that you enter this Temple in the 0=0 Grade, you part with all knowledge which you can attain through the five senses or any reasoning from these, and you seek to penetrate into the domain of the causes which lie beyond—the concealed Majesty of GOD. Now, here in the 0=0 Grade, you stand as it were, upon the threshold, as you might be standing between the doorposts of the doors and looking in. So stand you, in that 0=0 Grade between the Pillars which are symbolically called the *Immeasurable Region,* which you will remember, in this grade which we have just conferred upon you, the Very Honoured Hierophant invites you to enter as you stand between the Pillars.

Now, between the time that you enter the 0=0 Grade and the time you pass into this Grade, you have to study and be examined upon a certain Knowledge Lecture, of that knowledge I spoke somewhat in speaking of the 0=0 Grade. There is no need to say more about it now, but in that Knowledge Lecture you learned the names and the translation of the names of the Ten Sephiroth, and tenth of these you will remember was Malkuth, and the English translation of Malkuth is the *Kingdom.* And I daresay a shade of wonderment may have come over you as to why Malkuth, the *Kingdom*, is the tenth. The natural man says within himself—*surely the Kingdom is the highest thing to aspire to?* When you attain the *Kingdom* that is all that can be desired or aimed at. How then comes Malkuth to be the Tenth Sephirah?

Well consider for a moment what is a *kingdom* without a *king?—and in the days before there was a king is Israel, there reigned the Kings of Edom, the Lords of Forces.* Now Malkuth is the *kingdom,* it is true, but the *Kingdom of Hell.* It is the lowest of the ten Sephiroth and it represents the *material world.* It represents the human constitution, the material, the physical, tangible body, which we share with all vertebrate animals. Now, what is the duty of MAN? MAN was created by GOD ALMIGHTY, *a living soul,* and his duty is to enter into his kingdom as a king, there to sit as a king enthroned in his kingdom.

Now that is precisely the lesson which is taught you in this Grade of 1=10. You are shown in symbolic language (in algebraic language as I may put it to you) how that process is to be accomplished. You are shown also a synthesis in symbol of the material body and also of all material bodies. Because the Hermetic axiom holds here as it holds everywhere *as is above so below,* and his process is precisely the same whether it be the entry of a God into a planet, hitherto unoccupied and dead into his kingdom, whether it be the entry of the soul of man to take possession of his body, and to rule there as a King upon his throne, or whether it be man himself (that is afterwards) operating by magical power and taking possession of and influencing and ruling other bodies as a king upon his throne, whether it be the process of Alchemy which takes possession of the base matter and transmutes it into gold, or whether it be the influence of the Thaumaturge entering into the heart of nature and proclaiming changes there, it matters not; the formula is the same, and that formula is given, absolutely given in full in this grade which you have just passed through. Now, to guard against any disappointment that might occur from large promises and larger indications of this kind, I may tell you that it is very little indeed that I can tell you now—it is very little that I know myself—and that little the nature is such that if I might tell it to you it would be wholly unintelligible in your present stage of advance, because while you are yet in the *Outer,* much of this language must be sealed language to you, and even if I might utter it, it would fall upon absolutely deaf ears.

But what I can do is to call your attention to prominent parts of the Ritual, and show you things which perhaps many of you may have passed over without noticing, and I hope to lead you to search out further matters of thought for yourselves.

### *Symbolism of the Temple*

Now you will notice that the arrangement of the Temple is considerably different in this Grade from what it was when you were admitted to the 0=0. The Hegemon no longer sits between the Pillars, the Pillars are no longer placed in the East, but placed to the West of the Altar. The Black Banner of the West no longer stands beside the Hiereus, but it stands beside the Hierophant. And here I may mention one thing that may be of use to you. Always notice whenever the Black Banner changes its position and whenever you find the Black Banner in a different part of the Temple it signifies a bar of some kind.

Now, you have been told that this Grade represents the tenth Sephirah of Malkuth, the Kingdom. You must look upon yourself as the *spirit of man* for the first time entering his body, but that he is the lord and ruler of it, and that if he allow his body in any way to dominate his will he is a king abdicating his throne. Take that conception first, because in the words that were inscribed on the Portal of the Greek temple *Know Thyself,* in your own self you will find the key to all mysteries. Look therefore upon the temple as an algebraic symbol of your own bodies, and look upon the Neophyte entering the temple as your

own Divine Spirit, informed by your own Divine Will, entering
to take possession of the Kingdom of which God has given you.
Therefore, here, as in the 0=0, it is Hegemon (the representative of the Pillar of Mercy, the the Path of Goodness, and the
Synthesis of Equilibrium) who comes to bring you in. It is the
equilibrium of the body, the perfect poise which is at peace with
all the World, and therefore the representative of mercy, which
brings the Divine Spirit. When the body is as poised, then the
Spirit can enter.

## Advancement: First Part

So it is the Hegemon who is properly and necessarily our
leader, but it is the Sentinel, the Watcher Without, who prepares you to enter. Blindfolded, the King enters upon his Kingdom, blindfolded because he must have faith. By knowledge he
can never enter; by pride of Will, by pride of accomplishments or
attainments he can never enter; for man may study his whole
life, he may attain riches and honour, but never by these means
can be attain to the Kingship of his own body, but only by faith.
Therefore he enters the Temple blindfolded, and it is not the
Hegemon, representing mercy and Equilibrium, but it is the
Sentinel who keeps and guards the door without, who thus prepares him. And as he enters, it is the *Kerux*, the Announcer,
who bears the message to the body that the King is coming, who
opens the door. So the body, perfectly equiposed and at peace,
becomes aware that its king is entering.

Now, the *Hierophant* and the *Chiefs of the Temple,* sitting on
the Dais, represent to you the power of the recondite and occult,
powers beyond anything you can see, know, or conceive at present, they have emerged through the Veil from the concealed
Mystery of the Inner, of the Second Order: Therefore within the
Body of Man it is the indwelling Spirit of God who is to you as
the Chiefs of our temple, the Chiefs of the temple of your Body.
Therefore the *human spirit* enters upon that Temple of your
body, silent in reverence, *the Divine Spirit of GOD* indwelling
and permeating that Temple. Then as you enter the Temple

comes the solemn warning of the Hierophant: "Except the ADONAI build the House their labour is but lost that build it: except ADONAI keep the City the Watchman watches but in vain." Another exhortation to faith, because unless the Divine Spirit blesses you and makes you prosper, you may strive forever and you will never attain the smallest step, but if that assistance and blessing be granted, then everyone, no matter how weak, no matter how feeble, how erring, may aspire to the Kingship of the Kingdom of Malkuth.

There again comes the lesson of faith. No matter then how slow be your progress, no matter how frequent be your stumbles and falls, if ADONAI builds the House, the house will be built, and with the blessing of ADONAI your Spirit, informed by human Will, must at length sit upon the Throne of the human body.

Then does the Hierophant inquire why, by what aid, you seek admission to this Grade. The answer is *five-fold*—the Mystic Pentagram again. There are five aids:

*First* and almost always by the guidance of ADONAI, for without that you can do nothing.

*Secondly,* by the possession of the requisite knowledge. The knowledge you must have, but it profits nothing without the guidance of ADONAI.

*Thirdly,* by dispensation. That shows that not only is it the guidance of ADONAI that you trust to, but a permission which has come from behind the Veil to allow that King to enter upon his Kingdom. And in the human body that dispensation is represented by the Will to succeed in attaining Kingship of the Body.

*Fourthly,* you seek admission by the Secret Signs, Tokens of the 0=0 Grade. Something of this you know already and much more you will learn hereafter. You know already on entering the 0=0 Grade you are as a blind man groping in darkness. You step as one entering a threshold. You place the finger on the lips as vowing Silence and invoke the name of the GOD OF SILENCE, HAR-PAR-KRAT. There is much more in this than you know, but so much is sufficient for the present. By these signs of humility, of groping, of seeking for wisdom, of promised silence, you ask admission.

And *lastly,* of the symbol of the Hermetic Cross I shall speak a little later on. The Sign of the Hermetic Cross is peculiarly appropriate to this Grade, and there is little more than that may be said about it beside what was said by the Hierophant in explaining this symbol. And of course I must also ask you to remember that although I am taking the symbology of this Grade with reference to your own bodies, this symbology represents also the World, it represents also the Solar System, and you can as easily translate this symbology by imaginary light, and therefore Divine Guidance and planetary Gods coming into a dead planet such as the moon (which is an assumption of Kingship), as you can take the material body and the coming in of a king.

The Hierophant asks for the step, sign and grip of the Neophyte. For the present it is sufficient for you to take that to mean that you must give a visible and tangible evidence of having passed that Grade and it is only then that you are placed between the Pillars. Now, you remember that I told you that the Pillars are *the Portals of Occult Knowledge*—the Mystic Gateway. The *Portals* are hung up here on the East Wall and I shall come to them presently. But wherever you see those two Pillars you know that there is the Gateway, and you will notice as you go through the other Grades that every time you enter this Temple for a fresh grade the position of the Pillars will vary— sometimes they will be in one corner, sometimes in another, sometimes beside the South Wall. They will be in various places, and you must notice these, particularly with reference to other parts of the Temple, and observe that *there* is the gateway of Occult Science.

Now, in this particular Grade the Pillars stand to the West of the Altar, and you are placed between them, facing the cubical Altar of the Universe, still blindfolded. In faith, therefore you reach the portal of the *Immeasurable Region,* and from thence as a king surveying his kingdom, you must imagine your spirit, guided by your Will, looking towards the material part of our body, your own *material universe* in fact, symbolized by the cubical Altar in front of you: and in that position you pledge yourself—a king coming to take possession of his kingdom must indeed take the Coronation oath—you pledge yourself to adhere firmly to the same strict secrecy which you have previously vowed to maintain, and you swear by that kingdom which you are coming to take possession of, you swear by the earth on which you kneel.

After taking the Salt you begin to see. The hoodwink is removed and you see the temple. You see that the lights upon the Altar are unshaded, showing that you have passed from darkness into light. Then you take a few grains of Salt from the platter and scatter them towards the North. The North is the region of cold and darkness and is also the side of the Black Pillar of severity, and the North is also the side from which the powers of Earth operate upon the Temple. You say, "Let the Powers of Earth witness my Pledge" and then have to be purified again as before. Now the Hierophant speaks directly to you after having tested you and received your path. You are told what this kingdom consists of, under the symbology of the Garden of Eden. "TETRAGRAMMATON ELOHIM planted a garden eastward in Eden," and further than that there were two trees in it: (1) the Tree of Life and (2) the Tree of the Knowledge of Good and Evil, and the last Tree is the one that has two Paths.

The two Paths are symbolised by the Two Pillars, and by the Hiereus and Hegemon, the Guardians of the paths. Now, when the king, the *Spirit of man,* enters into his body, determined to rule there, the two paths are presented to him. He can rule in one way or he can rule in another. He can guide that body voluntarily outward into the outer darkness, away from the Light of GOD into pure matter and separation from GOD. And mind, this is kingship too, it is not the yielding to the body, but is is definitely and by determined design carrying the body along the path of separateness. This is the *kingship of the Devil.*

Now, the *Spirit of Man* which enters blindfolded, knowing

only good, knowing nothing of the distinction of good and evil, will first endeavour the path of separateness, that is always, since the fall of Man, the first impulse towards separateness, and towards the *kingdom of the Devil.* The Hidden Knowledge appears to be best attained in that way, because the "Wisdom of the Devil" is that GOD has hidden this knowledge from jealousy, so that MAN should become as GOD.

That was the voice of the Tempter in Eden, and it has been the voice of the tempter ever since. But there stands the Great Angel Samael, blocking the way, and from that moment that the Hiereus puts on the form of that Great Angel and stops the soul progressing on the path of Evil when he says, "Return, for thou canst not pass me by." The Neophyte then returns back to the threshold where the journey begins again only this time on the path of good, though here again he is warned back by the angel Metatron, for it is nigh on impossible for the Soul of man to go on by that Light. The wise man gazes upon the material universe and beholdeth therein the luminous image of the Creator. "Not as yet canst thou bear the dazzling radiance of that Light." So, then, you see, before the Soul of Man lie two things, both of which are barred from access. The weak and foolish man gazes upon the face of nature and beholds therein nothing but confusion because he has not the faith in GOD which enables him to see the equilibrium in the apparent disharmony. The wise man gazes upon the face of nature and beholds GOD through His Outer garments, but that vision is not for the Neophyte yet. Then there is an *alternative,* and the Hierophant says once more, "Let the Neophyte enter the Straight and narrow path which inclineth neither to the right hand nor to the left," the path of absolute equilibrium. And as he would enter upon this Path, Samael and Metatron, the keepers of the paths of good and Evil bar his way. The Hierophant steps down, the image of the Divine Spirit which is in him, whose sceptre draws down from the Eternal Uncreated Light, a ray with which to luminate the darkness of the material universe, and with that sceptre of Power he strikes asunder the weapons of the two angels who guard the Paths and allows the Neophyte to enter by this pathway, the feminine power and the power of mercy who prepares the pathway into the Light Divine. Only by sceptre of power and by the Divine Life, it is possible that the Neophyte can enter the *Immeasurable region* and only by that Divine Spirit dwelling in him can the Spirit of Man attain to the lordship of the kingdom of his body.

Thus you see the obstacles that intercept your path as you strive to obtain the mastery over the material body. It is a difficult task and the more you meditate upon the symbology of this temple as it is arranged or this Grade and upon the words which are spoken by the different officers, the more you will see how your spirit has to get in obtaining mastery over your body, how the king has to obtain his rightful throne.

So the Hierophant having thus thrust aside the opposing forces and interposed for you, shows the Flaming Sword and the Cherubim which are placed in the Garden of Eden to keep the way to the Tree of Life open. It is the Tree of Life to which you are aspiring, and the Tree of Life these ten Sephiroth whose names you in this Zelator Grade have learnt, and whose arrangement you now proceed to learn. You are also told the Signs and secrets of this Grade. As there is a great deal in these Signs you can be told now some of their significances.

You should always be able to remember the Sign of the *Interposer* as you give that Sign in remembrance and recognition of the interposition of the Hierophant for you. Therefore you should remember in giving this sign you are recognising and recalling remembrance the sceptre of power bringing down the Divine ray, the Spirit of GOD dwelling in you which interposed to allow the King of the Body to approach his rightful throne.

ADONAI HA ARETZ, the Grand Word, means "Lord of the Earth" in your own body, and not allowing the kingdom to dominate the King. The Password *Nun Heh* refers to an "ornament." "I will bind ye for an ornament upon my hand and for frontlets between my eyes," saith the Lord. The Material Body, the temple of the Holy Spirit, is indeed an ornament worthy of God Almighty, when dominated and ruled by the Divine Spirit which is the King of the body. Therefore *Nun Heh,* the ornament, is a very fitting password.

Now we come to the Three Portals. We cannot here (as they did in ancient Egypt) pass from Temple to temple through mighty stone Portals, therefore all we do is symbolically represent them, and these Three Portals are the three gates through which successively you will pass to attain any higher grades of this order. Remember therefore that to attain any higher grade or knowledge, always must you return to Malkuth. Whatever knowledge, whatever power you attain yourselves, in the world, though you attain to the very highest adeptship that ever yet was gained by man, the commencement is with your own body. Unless you can be lord of that you are a slave to it. Those Three Portals bear the Hebrew letters of Tau, Shin and Qoph. The purpose of these will be explained later as you study the Tree of Life though for the present remember that these three Hebrew letters make up the word *Quesheth* which means bow, the rainbow of promise. Therefore remember that when the king sits on the throne of the body, before him is the rainbow of promise. There are no heights to which he may not attain when that first step has been attained. In the 0=0 Grade you did not see these Portals which are now visible to you. In the 0=0 Grade you were only at the threshold, you looked upon the kingdom, as it were, which you were hereafter to conquer and rule, you now so promise.

Now symbolically you enter upon to commence to rule your body, so you see the rainbow of promise placed before you, which should be kept in your minds. On the Altar you will see the white triangle which again represents those paths which these Portals communicate, and the red cross is life and life within light, is upon the upper side of the altar.

One more point is shown to you in the first part of the 1=10 Grade, and that is the *Great Terrestrial Watch Tower* or the tablet of the North. At present it will probably be to all of you who are present, with the exception of those who have passed into the Second Order, an absolute sea of mystery. It appears a curious arrangement of squares and letters in different columns, and perhaps you may wonder to see the English and not the Hebrew Letters upon it, seeing that it is one of the most ancient symbols known in the world. I may tell you, that without betraying any knowledge that is beyond you that these letters are simply transliterated for convenience. I do not think that anyone present in the Temple except myself who read the original language though I may tell you this, that it is a great curiosity, merely from a linguistic point of view, because there is no record of the original characters nor am I aware that this language was ever spoken or these characters used by mortal man. Now that Muller and other great philologists have said that it is impossible that any human being should invent a language, yet here is a language that has existed for as far back as we have been able to trace. One will be able to find traces of it on rock cut Pillars and on temples apparently as old as the world itself but we find no trace of it as ever having been used as a living language and we hold a tradition that it is the angelic *secret language.* Only one instance of this I may be allowed to give. The high priest of Jupiter in the early days of Rome was called *Flamen Dialis.* They will tell you that it is ancient Etruscan, but beyond that they can tell you nothing. It is not the generative of any nominative. On that tablet you will see the second of the Three Holy Names of God is Dial.

Now, that the tablet represents EARTH, the four tablets represent the Four Elements, and the names of the characters upon them are the key to the power ruling the Elements. They are not placed in the temple to be understood, they cannot be understood, but they do exercise an occult power that they operate, or rather I should say (because no dead thing ever could exercise occult power) they operate as the focus of the Will brought through the Inner Order, which is behind the officers working this temple.

The Fylfot cross represents, as you know, the twelve signs of the Zodiac, and if you look at it carefully you will find that the twelve Signs are arranged along the arms in their four Triplicities, and they are put, not in the form of the cross, which is stationary, but in the form of the Swastika, which represents whirlings. Therefore the Fylfot Cross represents the whirling of the wheel of the Zodiac around the earth, disposed in its four triplicities, related to the Four Elements, showing you that the Kingdom, the body which you have come to rule, is not a fixed and solid thing, but is in perpetual motion and it is those motions that you have to rule. You are not expected to find it always the same, but always different. Just as you find the Wheel of the Zodiac up in the heavens different every moment you look at it, so will you find the elements in your own body different at every moment. Sometimes the fiery elements will be uppermost, sometimes the Water, but whatever it is you carry in your hand, you carry the *Spirit* of the Immortal Emanation, from GOD Almighty for you carry the *whirling Elements* in your hand, and that is your badge of admission to our kingdom. Whatever way they whirl around you, which ever is uppermost, it may be Fire, Water, Earth or Air, no matter, you must rule it. You must carry in your hand and hold it any way you please as only you can be King of your own body.

## *Second Part*

Now, if you have appreciated the symbology so far, the second portion may be very soon dealt with. You have learnt what your body is, what the Kingdom is that you have to enter to rule. Now you have to sit down upon the throne thereof, and the symbology is taken from the Temple of Jerusalem. As Saint Paul said: "Know ye that your bodies are the temple of the Holy Ghost?" In fact you are the Divine SPIRIT and Keeper of the Temple, pledged to God Almighty not to allow any profanation thereof, pledge to keep that temple pure and clean and fit for the habitation of the HOLY SPIRIT, whose Temple it is. Therefore you are taught now how to enter the Holy place as a priest of the temple. Heretobefore as King you enter your Kingdom, now as a priest you enter the Holy Place of your Temple. Outside stood the *Altar of Burnt Offerings* whereon were sacrificed the various animals. What are these animals? All our evil and animal passions. Everything in our human body which we share with the animals, any desire to eat, to drink, or anything else, must be sacrificed. That means not that the human needs of the body must be neglected. In olden times when these things were better understood, although animals were offered in sacrifice, animals were used in material things. Because the Jew of old offered oxen for burnt offering it did not prevent his ploughing the land with his oxen; he was commanded to do so. So all our material passions must be offered in sacrifice, but must also be made to subserve our material needs that we may rule them and not allow them to rule us.

Then purify with Fire and purify with Water; then again the Signs must be given. You must grope in your darkness and pledge yourselves to silence. You must recall the Divine interposer who admitted you to your and avow yourself to be an ornament of almighty. Then you may come once more to stand on the threshold of the Holy Palace, and pass through the threshold to the Holy Place in the sign of the Interposer.

Now then you see the *nature of the Throne* you have come to occupy. On the *North Side* was the *Table of Shewbread* and there were the twelve loaves upon it, which symbolised the Twelve Signs of the Zodiac, the Wheel of Life which is steady now because you now rule them, offered up on that table for GOD Almighty. And these Signs of the Zodiac refer to every part of the human body, from Aries which is the head, to Pisces which is the feet. Every Sign has its particular location in the human body; therefore the whole human body lies there upon the Table of Shewbread upon the North Side, offered up to the King of Kings. And on the South Side in the *Seven Branched Candle Stick*—the seven Planets, the Wanderers, the Wandering Lights, the Wandering Influences of MAN, which pass from Sign to Sign, from point to point in his body, his mind, his life, his dominating and governing principles, again all placed in the complete circle and offered up to the Lord who governs motion, and Lord of the North. He governs rest and darkness and silence—only two aspects of the one living God of Heaven. The Seven Planets, Seven Churches, Seven days of the Week, all mystic sevens that are symbolised by the Seven Branched Candle stick, the Seven Light Bearers, are offered here.

Then *Eastward* of you is the veil, which hides the holy of Holies from which the Priests of the temple have emerged, and from you which the glory of Hod shines upon you. And in front of the Temple veil stands the Altar of Incense hence the incense ascends like a prayer to the Throne of God, as you may imagine the Veil of the Holy of Holies stretched behind us here, and you may imagine our forms as those of Divine persons emerged from behind that Veil, or looking at your own body behind the SPIRIT of Prayer which is upon the Altar of Incense, the prayers which you offer to the Divine, you may imagine such manifestations as may be allowed you of the Divine SPIRIT, itself emerged from the Veil which shrouds the Holy of Holies from your Soul's gaze. Now, the Altar, as you are told, is black, but the Altar of Incense in the Temple of Solomon was gold. Why black? Because you are in Malkuth, because black is the colour of Earth, and as I told you, however high you rise you will have to come back to Malkuth always, and the body, the Malkuth of yourselves is a perishing body. Black is the colour of putrefaction, and death must result to this earthly body of ours, therefore is the Altar Black. And the Fire and the Water and the Incense are upon it. Receptive you must be as Water, energetic must you be as Fire, and your prayers like smoke of the incense must rise up to the Throne of God.

So you must learn from this to govern *your own body*. That is the first lesson which is taught to you. And as you proceed you will find that by and by that the same principle which enabled you to govern your own body enables you to obtain any knowledge you want, to produce and effect want to produce and the whole thing lies within the compass of this 1=10 Grade of which I can only give you the very faintest and simplest outline. I have told you nothing new, it is all in the ritual, but perhaps I may have succeeded in calling your attention to some things you may have passed over, because inattention is one of the greatest barriers that keep us from self development.

# B1

## Lectures and Addresses
## of the 1=10 Grade of Zelator
## Whare Ra Temple

# 1

# The 1=10 Ceremony

Self-Development, in some form or another, may be said to be that which we are seeking, that for which we are associated together. For unless we have some real and earnest purpose behind what we do, these Ceremonies are mere Burlesques and unworthy of our attention. But by joining the Order and attending its Ceremonies and undergoing its training, we hope to make ourselves better men and women than we were. We also hope to gain a further knowledge of the inner secrets of Nature, so that we may be able to use those powers of Nature whose existence we are conscious of, but whose modes of operation are hidden from materialism and which are therefore called "occult." In our quest the Order helps in many ways. First of all, the Chiefs of the Temple, and to a lesser degree all Members of the Inner Order, can and do help occultly all members of the Outer Order from the Neophyte Grade up to that of 4=7.

There is another way in which this Order helps you, and that is by its Ceremonies, and by the symbolism of its Ceremonies: that is what we are concerned with in this Lecture. As you gradually come to understand the symbolism of Grade after Grade you will find that you are really learning formulae for your own development. Having learnt how to apply these formulae to yourself you can then apply them to the influencing for good of the outer world.

Remember that of the ten squares constituting the Cubical Altar in the center of the Temple only one and that the one on which it stands, represents the utmost part of the "material universe" of which you can have knowledge by what are termed the senses, and that, from the position of the Altar, is hidden. Therefore you are bidden, at the very beginning of this 1=10 Ceremony, to "enter the immeasurable region," to penetrate into the domain of the causes which lie beyond the material universe, to seek the concealed Majesty of GOD.

Now this Grade is referred to Malkuth, the Kingdom, the lowest of the Ten Sephiroth: it represents the material, the physical, the human constitution: It is your duty to enter into your Kingdom as a King, and there to sit enthroned as a King in his Kingdom: this is the lesson of the 1=10 Grade. The Kingdom is in fact the physical body, and the Kingship is the absolute control of this body. In ordinary life control of the body is necessary, but in the occult life it is far more so.

The outstanding feature of the first part of the Ceremony was your choice of one of the three pathways. That of "Good" may have seemed the natural one to have chosen, but it was barred for it is impossible to live the entirely spiritual life in the flesh. The true path, you were told finally, is the middle one, to live a true and upright life but not rejecting the material plane. Equilibrium, perfect control, is necessary before the King can really reign in his Kingdom. Remember the Hierophant's solemn warning:—"Except ADONAI builds the house their labour is but lost that build it." We of ourselves can do nothing.

The admission badge, the whirling Swastika, or Fylfot Cross, symbolically resumes this idea of control. The whirling of the Zodiac, disposed in four Triplicities, related to the four Elements, shows that the Kingdom, the body, which you have to rule, is not a fixed and solid thing but that it is in perpetual motion. Whatever way it may whirl, whatever element may be uppermost in you, you must rule it: so only can you be King of your own body.

The second part of the Ceremony takes its symbology from the Temple at Jerusalem and carries this lesson of ruling the body a step further. As a King you entered your Kingdom, now as a Priest you enter the Holy Place. On the Altar of Burnt Offering are to be sacrificed our animal passions: but though offered in sacrifice they must be made to subserve our material needs so that we may rule them and not allow them to rule us. Then on the North side or the Holy Place was the Table of Shewbread. The twelve loaves are the Twelve Signs of the Zodiac and these again refer to the twelve parts of the human body: therefore the whole human body lies there offered up in sacrifice On the South side was the Seven-branched Candlestick: the seven Planets or the seven senses. The whole of the symbology then points to the ruling of the Kingdom, the governing of the body. As you proceed you will find that the same principle which enabled you to govern your own body will enable you to obtain any knowledge you want, to produce any effect you want to produce: the whole thing lies within the compass of this 1=10 Grade.

One or two other points in connection with this 1=10 Ceremony may be noted. As the Grade is referred to Earth and deals with the physical body, therefore the Earth Spirits or Gnomes are invoked at the opening, and these may be seen by those who are clairvoyant during the Ceremony. Similarly at the subsequent Grades the other Elementals are invoked in turn. This is not for any idle display of magical power, far from it. By these Ceremonies the Elementals are definitely aided in their spiritual progress, so in addition to them helping us, we are helping them.

Then finally come to the "Three Portals." We are not able to do as they used to do in Ancient Egypt, pass from Temple to Temple through mighty stone portals. Therefore we symbolically represent them by the Hebrew Letters, and they are the gates through which you must pass to attain a higher Grade.

Remember that however high you attain you must always return to Malkuth. The commencement is within your own body: unless you are Lord of that you can be Lord of nothing. The Three Portals in the 1=10 are ‫קסת‬, making the word Queseth, the Rainbow of Promise, Now, having entered the Kingdom which is to be conquered and ruled, you have before you the promise, and limitless is the height to which you may attain when once you have crossed the threshold. Again remember the warning:—"Except ADONAI build the house their labour is but lost that build it."

# 2

# The Rituals and How to Read Them

At the first hearing the Rituals of the Grades of the Outer Order may seem to some to be almost incomprehensible. It is certainly true that it is necessary to be a Member of the Inner or Second Order before a full grasp of their meaning can be obtained. For one thing, these Ceremonies do not take place on the physical plane only, they have their counterpart on the higher planes, Inability to grasp their full significance at once should be a stimulus rather than a bar to the study of them. Taken singly or as a consecutive whole, the Rituals will be found to be a veritable mine of information and an inexhaustible source of inspiration.

It must be borne in mind that, although during these Ceremonies you may fail to understand much of what is going on and may be mentally fogged by being shown a number of what to you are meaningless diagrams, yet every action, every diagram, has a definite effect upon your "sphere of Sensation," upon your aura, vivifying the symbols contained therein. This may not be noticeable to you at the time, but you will derive the benefit subsequently. These Rituals are intended to stimulate thought: they are full of tabloid information, camouflaged to a certain extent perhaps, if you like to use that term. But a prize which has to be striven for is valued more highly than an outright gift. Surface reading will yield but little: read and re-read, and come to the ceremonies to hear them read.

Before you have gone very far in your training you learn that "when rightly understood, the TREE OF LIFE is the key of all things." Consider, then, each Ritual in its relation to the Tree of Life: to which Sephira it refers. Consider also what Paths are trodden during the Ceremony, the admission badges and their symbolism and the general purport of the various diagrams which you are shown. Look up in a dictionary or elsewhere the various classical allusions: if a Mason, compare with Masonic degrees: in general, seek out all correspondences.

After generalities go through each Ritual, endeavouring to identify yourself with each officer in turn, In the opening part of the 0=0 Ritual the names of the Officers and the nature of their Offices is set forth at length. Ascertain therefore how in each Ceremony the Officers do carry out the functions attributed to them: consider each officer's actions as well as words—the effect which they would have on you as that officer and also their relation to the candidate, Finally identify yourself with the candidate. Ponder on what he experiences when hoodwinked, and then what he experiences when the symbol of blindness is removed—and this right through the Ceremony. What influence should each Ceremony have upon the Candidate, and what symbols should be vivified in his sphere of sensation? Naturally to do this thoroughly will take time, but nothing worthwhile is ever attained without effort. If the Rituals are conscientiously studied, the taking of an Office at a Ceremony, instead of being a case for nervous prostration, will be a joy and a privilege and the subsequent writing of a thesis upon the Outer Rituals (a thing expected later on of all candidates) will not be the cause of confusion.

# 3

# Thinking Backwards

"Thinking backwards" is a piece of training that will assist you in many ways; will strengthen your mind, memory and will-power.

Every night for a few minutes before retiring to bed, make yourself comfortable in an easy chair, with your back to the North and with your feet warm. Then start thinking backward right through the day, taking incident by incident in order until you reach the time when you awoke in the morning. Don't go into too much detail at first: let the day pass before you as a cinematograph film, the incidents etc. taking place in the reverse order to that in which they actually occurred. With practice you will be able to go back through several days, then weeks, and finally years; it needs no imagination to see the value of being able to recall what you are doing or saying at any past time.

Eight hours out of every twenty-four, for one third of your life, you are asleep and normally do not know what you are doing. During that time your subconscious self is looking after your body helping it to recuperate. Having done this, the subconscious self goes and meets the Higher Self, transferring to it the sum total of the day's events, thus you are constantly character building outside yourself, If you train yourself to think backwards the time will come when you will be able to ascertain what you were doing ere you awoke, to have knowledge of the subconscious life during sleep when the subconscious self is not in the body. Finally you may learn of your last and previous lives, of when you made your first choice of incarnation.

There is a Trinity above and below: before you entered this world you were three points in a circle, At birth two of these incarnated in the physical body prepared for you—your mind and your subconscious mind, The other point, your Higher Self, stayed outside, connected with the physical body by a very thin attenuated line of etheric substance. The base line of a triangle is made between the brain or waking consciousness and the subconscious self. During sleep the subconscious self is in contact with the Higher Self, forming the base and one side of the triangle. The third side of the triangle we formulate for you at the 0=0. In time you may be able to draw down your Higher Self to converse with you, and so find out whence you came, why you are here at all, and what your real object in this life is. Surely it is worthwhile to find this out, to have a certainty, rather than a pious hope or idea, as to the past, present, and may be the future too, if GOD wills.

# 4

# The Hebrew Alphabet

*by M.C. (Mrs. R. W. Felkin)*

In giving our students the Hebrew Alphabet to study we are taking them back to the foundations of the intellectual tradition of the present day. To understand this it is necessary for us to glance back to the beginning of human history. We have reason to believe that humanity in its present form was evolved on the antediluvian continent of Atlantis and that at the submergence of this continent offshoots of their civilisation survived in those races which we know as the Egyptian, the Caucasian and the Celtic. There were also the forerunners of the Mongolian. Here, then, we have those primitive races who first reduced the spoken word to the written symbol. Celtic origins are still veiled in obscurity, but the remaining three reveal themselves to the patient investigation of the archaeologist and etymologist as unbroken streams descending and branching out into the languages of today. With Mongolian tongues we have no concern, they are alien alike in sound, construction and written form. But from the Sanskrit of the Caucasian and the Egyptian are derived the modern tongues of the greater part of the present civilisation.

There can be but little doubt that when the wandering tribes of the Hebrews first settled in Egypt they had practically no written language. They spent, we are told, 400 years in the land of Goshen, that is approximately as long as from the time of Queen Elizabeth to the present day! When they first settled in the land of Goshen on the Eastern side of the Nile there were 70 people, including women and children. When they fled, four centuries later, their number is said to have been over six hundred thousand. It is reasonable to conclude that in the interval, although they remained separate from the natives of the country, yet they imbibed most of their customs and as much as possible of their language and learning. Moses, their leader, was brought up by the priests and initiated into their mysteries. He was familiar with their system of hieroglyphics and there can be but little doubt that when he set himself the stupendous task of recording the history of Israel he availed himself of both the form of writing and much of the cosmogony which he had acquired in his temple training. By this means he was enabled to preserve the inner tradition while at the same time presenting an exoteric history. For it is the peculiarity of the genius of both Egyptian Hieroglyphics and of the Hebrew writing that it is capable of a three-fold interpretation, literal, symbolic and spiritual.

In studying the actual letters as we now possess them we must of course admit that they have undergone a considerable modification since the days of Moses, the most important being their approximation to the Chaldean owing to the exile. From the Chaldean also was borrowed the vocalisation system by means of points placed above, below, or within a letter. Nevertheless the hieroglyphic idea is retained in that each letter represents not merely a sound, but also an object, and the name of the letter is also the name of the object, hence the list which you were given in the First Knowledge Lecture. That is to say— ALEPH (Arabic, ALIF) not only means the letter A or E (or more accurately, the opening of the mouth to make a sound), it is also the name of an ox. The word BETH is not only the letter B or V, but it is also the name of a house.

There is another thing you have to bear in mind. In all the ancient languages there was only one system of notation for both sound and number. Therefore each letter is also a number and each word has a numerical value equal to the sum of its numbers. Thus אל is not only a sound EL or AL, and a Divine Name, it is also 30 plus 1 = 31.

Moreover a language like Hebrew had comparatively few words, but each word had numerous shades of meaning indicated either by the context or by the inflection and also each individual letter had its own essential meaning: therefore it follows that the word was the sum of or modification of those meanings, just as numerically it was the sum of those individual numbers. Thus אל which signifies the number 31, is formed from א the sign of power and from ל the sign of extension. Its spiritual meaning is therefore Extended Power, and hence GOD, the Power extended over all. Used in a restricted or materialised sense it may be translated as towards, against, upon. The same letters reversed לא represent spiritually the prolongation of movement to infinity, which translated upon a lower plane becomes a negative and may be rendered as no, not.

Let us now consider the abstract symbolism of each of these letters.

א is the sign of power, stability, unity. It represents mankind as ruler of the earth. ALEPH = an ox.

ב is interior action. It represents virility, and an interior, a dwelling place. BETH = a house. Unite these two and you have אב or אבא, a father.

ג is the sign of organic development, hence the throat, or a canal which organises or controls inflexion of sound, a glass of water. GIMEL = a camel.

ד is the sign of abundance from division, divisible nature, the source of physical existence: the breast, source of nourishment. The word DALETH signifies a door, the entrance or exit.

ה This letter merits special attention. It is the symbol of Universal Life, the breath. It be translated as either E or H and is closely akin to ה in meaning as well as form. It is frequently used as an article, and may be translated as the, this, that, of. In this aspect it is used as a prefix or as an affix. It forms when united with a vowel sound the principal Deity Names and in this aspect it indicates an abstraction which no modern language can render adequately. Thus יה is Absolute Life, Eternal, Immutable. אהיה can only be adumbrated as That Which Is—Was—Will be. It is the root of the verb To Be, to exist, and is used to denote the source of human life in the Name היה which we translate as EVE, but which also may be given as HUA the third person singular of the verb To Be, or simply as HE. When the significant י is added it becomes Tetragrammaton יהוה, the Inviolable Name which must not be taken in vain and which was only intoned by the High Priest upon entering the Holy of Holies. Even today no orthodox Jew attempts to utter it.

ו This letter is equivalent to O, U or V. It is therefore convenient to use the point to indicate the sound since its symbolism differs widely according to its pronunciation. As a V ו is used as a conjunction and is placed at the beginning of a word; it may be translated as and, also, thus, then, afterwards; but it links words together more intimately than any of these. Used as a vowel, ו = O, ו = U or OU, it is then a sign of action and has the peculiarity of transforming a verb from the present to the past or from the past to the future. In these aspects it no longer represents the junction of two things (as an hook and an eye, a knot, a link), rather it is the symbol of light, sound, air, wind. Hence רוח = the wind, breath or soul, because ר = movement, ח = life, and ו in the midst gives the peculiar human character to the word which indicates expansion, inspiration.

ז The hissing sound of something passing through the air, hence a sword or arrow, a javelin or spear. It also denotes the refraction of light, suggesting the dazzling appearance of a ray of light falling on polished metal. It may be transliterated as Z, C or S.

ח This letter is closely allied to ה both in form and in significance; but as it is more closed in form so it is more guttural in sound and of a material connotation. It signifies life, but on a lower plane. It implies effort, labour, care. Thus in concrete example it indicates a field, an enclosure upon which labour must be expended.

ט hieroglyphically shows the coiled serpent protecting her eggs, hence the universal tradition of the serpent guarding treasure. From that we get the idea of a shield, shelter, a roof protecting man's family as the serpent protects her eggs. Finally a haven, refuge or goal.

י Here we come to another profound symbol of deep significance. The hieroglyphlic interpretation is that of the hand. But it is a hand held out in action, thus it is the symbol of creation. It is the symbol of a flame detached from any material base, free, the leaping creative impulse. By a natural transition we get the phallic symbol of creative power. On the abstract spiritual plane we have the Divine Creator. Thus this letter transmutes הי ה, the feminine source of life, into יהוה, the Ineffable Supreme.

כ Hieroglyphically this represents the closed or half-closed hand, a fist; hence a hollow, therefore a receptacle: the power of assimilation, reflection, meditation. It forms a link between ה the sign of manifest life and ג the sign of organisation, and carries in itself something of the symbolism of both these. Used as an article or preposition it may be translated as similar, according to. Vocalised by י it signifies כי and = because, for, then, when.

ל In a material sense this suggests any extension, the outstretched arm of man, the unfolded wing of a bird, hence the further symbolism of the whip lash or ox-goad. But when these interpretations are raised to the spiritual plane we perceive at once how significant this letter becomes. אל therefore, represents an Extension of Power, omnipotence. Hence אלהים is the Extension of the Power of Life to the nth degree, that aspect of the Divine which is capable of creating without effort. Conversely לא signifies an indefinite and therefore unknown and incalculable quantity, which brought down from the abstract to the concrete becomes negation, no, not.

מ The sign of plastic or passive action; the genuine protective aspect of creative power. Hence vocalised as מֵ׳ם it signifies water, always used in the plural since the final MEM is collective as water is the condensation of moisture. With the letter שׁ prefixed we get שָׁמַ׳ם, the Heavens, the ethereal water or atmosphere. Used as an article or prefix מ may be rendered as from, out of, with, among. Hieroglyphically we may say that מ indicates rough water, sea waves, while ם final suggests rather still, calm water.

נ This letter is the image of produced or reflected existence, offspring, fruit, a child; hence it represents hieroglyphically a fish, the inhabitant of water. Joined to ב the sign of interior action, it becomes בֶן, a son. This is more clearly defined when we realise that ן final is augmentative and emphasises the individuality. נ at the beginning of a word suggests passive action, contemplation folded in upon itself: ן at the end is the converse, unfolding. Thus נב represents inspiration, prophecy, ecstasy. From this is derived נבֵ׳א a prophet.

ס As it presents the development of the hissing sound of ז, so hieroglyphically it is the duplication, the duplicate link forms a prop, not merely joining but supporting. It is the image of all circular and spiral movement, possibly a deduction from the peculiar movement of the serpent.

ע Hieroglyphically this letter signifies an eye and here we find one of the most curious and erudite survivals of occult knowledge. Superficially there seems to be but little likeness between the letter and the symbol. When we come to consider it more carefully we find that it is indeed an extraordinary glyph of the organs of vision. Externally we have the two eyes ' ', but inside our head lies a small body, one (or rather two closely connected) of the so-called "ductless glands" of modern physiology—the pineal and the pituitary glands. These glands are connected with the external eyes by delicate nerves, and when the external eyes are exercised in certain methods they awake a definite response in the internal gland—the "third eye" of legend. The complete ע is an exact counterpart of the complete organism and signifies the whole visual apparatus. One of the secondary results is the reaction upon the general muscular system.

Phonetically ע represents the opening of the glottis (in the throat to make a guttural sound and therefore it is transliterated as AA- OO- WH- or NG. Thus it symbolises interior hollow sound or noise and connotes materialism or emptiness, sometimes falsity or perversity. It is the physical aspect of ו and when used as a consonant almost always has an evil implication.

פ, which is a hieroglyph of the open mouth, naturally symbolises speech. It is transliterated as either P, in which case it closely resembles ב in meaning as well as form, or as PH, in which case it approximates rather to the meaning of ו.

צ represents all ideas of severance, solution; concretely it represents the hook by which something may be caught or ended. In sound it falls into the same group as ז and ס, though it is harder and more abrupt. Placed at the beginning of words it indicates the movement which carries us on towards an end; placed at the end as ץ final it indicates the end accomplished: on a higher plane it represents a refuge for man.

ק This is another guttural and like ע it suggests a materialistic tendency. Hieroglyphically it represents an ear ק. Symbolically it becomes an implement or instrument by which man may accomplish an act or defend himself. It marks at once force and restraint. It is significant of repression and decision. In sound it is the harder and more guttural sound of ב. Abstractly we may trace a regular succession of descent and development. Thus ה = universal life, pure being; ח the life of nature, manifest existence; ב assimilated life-building natural form; and ק material existence giving the means of form.

ר This letter is par excellence the sign of movement. Hieroglyphically it is the head of man ראש which directs the movement of his whole body, a captain, or by a slight alteration in focus, the initiative movement which predicates life and ultimate form; the culminating point of all things. Hence

ראש הגלגלים, the vortex, the beginning of primeval movement, the Sphere of the Elements. It is the centre unfolding to
the circumference, the creative elemental fire: the renewal of all
by movement; the perpetual vibrations of ions building up matter. Hence אוֹר, fire, action, contrasted with אֵשׁ, potential fire.

שׁ is said to represent the teeth, by which its sound is produced. It completes the symbolism of ז and ם and is in a sense
bound to them, for as ז = the arrow and ם = the bowstring so
שׁ symbolises the bow itself; hence we are told that the Three
Paths on the Tree of Life form קֶשֶׁת, the Bow, the material sign
of reciprocity between God and man. שׁ is the symbol of movement and duration, Used as a prefix it communicates a double
power of movement and of conjunction. It may be pronounced
either SS or as SH and it usually has a point above it to indicate
which sound is to be used, שׂ = SS and שׁ = SH. Geometrically it
represents the semi-arc of circle, whereas ר is the straight forward movement of a radius and ם a spiral. By analysis we find
that the Divine Name שׁדִי represents the Overarching Heavens protecting the fecundity and abundance of Nature—hence
Providence.

ת The last letter of the Hebrew Alphabet, is a glyph of the
Cross, the name being still retained to indicate the ancient form
of Cross—the Tau T, sacred to THOOTH. It is probable indeed,
that the letter was originally written thus and gradually elabo-
rated to distinguish it from ר. It is the sign of reciprocity, of
that which is mutual, interchanging, sympathetic. Joined to the
first letter of the alphabet it indicates אֵת, the essence, the
inmost self of a thing or a person, and in this form it is repeatedly used by Moses as a prefix in his account of Creation to indicate that he is not describing a material or individual, but an
essential process which developed on a higher plane prelimi-
nary to any physical manifestation.

In analysing the various Names that occur in the Knowledge
Lectures and elsewhere, it must be remembered that each letter
modifies as well as emphasises the others; that the meaning of
the whole word is the combination, not the simple addition of its

constituents. But an intelligent appreciation of the wonderful symbolism contained in the 22 Letters of the Alphabet will go far towards helping us to gain an insight not only into the Hebrew but also into all other languages, since every super-structure must conform to its foundations. I may add that each letter has also been attributed to a portion of the human body, but as Astrology has accepted this system with regard to the Zodiacal and Planetary Signs it is better not to confuse the issues by dwelling upon this classification. Rather let us con-clude with the saying of the Rabbi—"In the Beginning GOD took the 22 Letters, and with them He formed, combined, and designed all that was made."

# The Second Knowledge Lecture
# Whare Ra Temple

The three Principles of Nature as addressed to their Alchemical aspects are:

| Sulphur | Mercury | Salt |
|---------|---------|------|
| 🜍 | ☿ | ⊖ |

The Metals attributed to the Planets are:

Lead ♄
Iron ♂
Gold ☉
Copper/Brass ♀
Quicksilver ☿
Silver ☽

SOL PHILOSOPHORUM: The Pure Living Alchemical Spirit of Gold; the refined essence of Heat and Fire.

LUNA PHILOSOPHORUM: The Pure Living Alchemical Spirit of Silver; the refined essence of Heat and Moisture.

GREEN LION: The Stem and Root of the Radical essence of Metals.

BLACK DRAGON: Death—Putrefaction—Decay.

KING: Red—The Qabalistic Microprosopus.
    Tiphareth—analogous to Gold and the Sun.

QUEEN: White—The Qabalistic Bride of the Microprosopus.
    Malkuth—analogous to Silver and the Moon.

THE FOUR ORDERS OF THE ELEMENTALS ARE:
    1. Spirits of Earth     GNOMES
    2. Spirits of Air       SYLPHS
    3. Spirits of Water     UNDINES
    4. Spirits of Fire      SALAMANDERS
These are the Essential Spiritual Beings called upon to praise GOD in the "Benedicite Omnia Opera."

The KERUBIM are the Living Powers of Tetragrammaton on the Material Plane and the presidents of the Four material Elements. They operate through the Fixed or Kerubic Signs of the Zodiac and are thus symbolised and attributed:

| Kerub of Air | Man | Aquarius | ♒ |
| Kerub of Fire | Lion | Leo | ♌ |
| Kerub of Earth | Bull | Taurus | ♉ |
| Kerub of Water | Eagle | Scorpio | ♏ |

TETRAGRAMMATON means Four-Lettered Name and refers to the Unpronounceable Name of God symbolised by Jehovah.

THE LAVER OF WATER OF PURIFICATION refers to the Waters of Binah, the Female Power reflected in the Waters of Creation.

THE ALTAR OF BURNT OFFERING for the sacrifice of animals symbolises the Qlippoth of Evil demons of the Plane contiguous to and below the Material Universe. It points out that our passions should be sacrificed.

THE QLIPPOTH are the Evil Demons of Matter and Shells of the Dead.

THE ALTAR OF INCENSE in the Tabernacle was overlaid with Gold. Ours is black to symbolise our work which is to separate the Philosophic Gold from the Black Dragon of Matter.

The Altar Diagram shows the Ten Sephiroth with all the connecting Paths numbered and lettered, and the serpent winding over each Path. Around each Sephirah are written the names of the Deity, Archangel, and Angelic Host attributed to it. The twenty-two Paths are bound together by the serpent of Wisdom. It unites the Paths but does not touch any of the Sephiroth, which are linked by the Flaming Sword. The Flaming Sword is formed by the natural order of the Tree of Life. It resembles a Lightning Flash.

The Two Pillars on the side of the Altar represent:
ACTIVE—WHITE PILLAR ON SOUTH SIDE.
> Male.
> Adam.
> Pillar of Light and Fire.
> Right Kerub.
> Metatron.

PASSIVE—BLACK PILLAR ON NORTH SIDE.
> Female.
> Eve.
> Pillar of Cloud.
> Left Kerub.
> Sandalphon.

THE FOUR WORLDS OF THE QABALAH ARE:
> Atziluth, Archetypal—Pure Deity.
> Briah, Creative—Archangelic.
> Yetzirah, Formative—Angelic.
> Assiah, Action—Matter, Man, Shells, Demons.

The Ten Houses, or Heavens of Assiah, the Material World are:
> 1. Primum Mobile, Rashith ha-Gilgalim.
> 2. Sphere of the Zodiac, Mazloth.
> 3. Sphere of Saturn, Shabbathai.
> 4. Sphere of Jupiter, Tzedek.

5. Sphere of Mars, Madim.
6. Sphere of Sol, Shemesh.
7. Sphere of Venus, Nogah.
8. Sphere of Mercury, Kokab.
9. Sphere of Luna, Levanah.
10. Sphere of the Elements, Olam Yesodoth.

The traditional Tarot consists of a pack of 78 cards made up of four suits of 14 cards each, together with 22 Trumps, or Major Arcana, which tell the story of the Soul. Each suit will consist of ten numbered cards, as in the modern playing cards, but there are four instead of three honours: King or Knight, Queen, Prince or King, Princess or Knave.

The Four Suits are:

1. Wands or Scepters comparable to Diamonds.
2. Cups or Chalices comparable to Hearts.
3. Swords comparable to Spades.
4. Disks or Coins comparable to Clubs.

# Evil

## by A.M.M. (R.W. Felkin)

I can remember quite well, about 28 years ago, going through this 1=10 ceremony myself. Then I think was the first time I ever realised what Evil was, and how thankful I was for it. I want you to get hold of the idea of Evil as opposing forces.

This 1=10 ceremony shows you three paths, either of which you might have chosen had you been left to yourself, these two paths being that of Good and Evil. A better road, the straight and narrow one, is ultimately pointed out to you as the one to be followed.

Now it is absolutely essential to have opponents to struggle against in order to develop a balanced nature. Think of life in that way and you will get much help. If it had not been for all the evil of the years of the war there would not have been the same chance for the materialization of all the good that which was developed and shown by those who were fighting and by those who were helping in other ways. Evil then is an opposing force which helps us towards the attainment of a balanced nature, and by overcoming that force we develop the opposite quality.

Before the candidate enters the temple for this ceremony the
Spirits of Earth are invoked and near the Northern Tablet are
the Elemental Gnomes. They are working for the world, and it
is our privilege to help them to a higher degree of Spiritual
power and utility; they too are struggling and striving for perfection, and in our ceremony we do aid them in their progress.
In subsequent ceremonies you will comes across the other Elementals in a similar way.

Remember, then, this is the Earth Grade, resembling the
physical body, bones and muscles. It also shows you that a
sound basis is necessary for the perfect development of a temple
for the Holy Spirit; your object and duty is to accomplish this as
far as possible.

After each ceremony, take and study the ritual, for it contains
so much that it would take literally weeks of study to really
grasp the whole of the cosmic knowledge and teaching in it. In
all sacred scriptures the words themselves are only the garment: get behind the text and study and meditate and really
penetrate what really lies behind. We know that the Bible tells
us that the creation was accomplished in six days, in a week
that is, and the dates given in the margin tell us that this took
place not many thousands of years ago. Yet we know from geol-
ogy and from other sources that the earth is five or six thousand
million years old; instead of "days" we must therefore understand years or long eras of time. One of these great eras is now
coming to an end, and the next begins when the Sun enters the
Sign of Aquarius.

Since the disturbing influence of the Great War, as well as
before it, there has been industrial unrest, all manners of striving and general wonderment as to what will happen next. An
increase of spiritual power must come and descend upon the
world: these are the Signs of the times. You will realise therefore the responsibility which rests upon you is very great, for
you have your part to play in the reconstruction of the world.
You have knowledge to spread, not that it means revealing of
Order Secrets, but so altering your lives and aspirations in the
light of what you are learning, you will be able to do good to all

with whom you may come into contact.

Whose fault is all the present industrial unrest? People do not realise that there must be give and take on both sides: and so it is in everything connected with this life, this is the only way of progress. Cultivate the balanced nature and let each do what he or she can towards spreading this idea amongst them.

# Symbology of the Gate

*by M.C. (Mrs. Felkin)*

You will notice that in this grade the Symbology of the Gate is constantly used: it is one of the most interesting and wonderful symbols in life, and as you study the rituals of the Order you will see that they are founded upon the Tree of Life, the Ten Sephiroth being joined by the twenty two paths, and in each grade there is a gateway to a higher stage or plane. We are told that our first parents were driven out of the gate of Eden, that is from the Higher plane to the Material plane, their coats of skin symbolising their physical bodies. Each of us must of necessity seek that gate in order to return whence we came.

As we pass along the road of life, we see many gates, which we want to open and look over, but we must be on our guard lest we follow the path of evil. There is a form of Black Magic which maintains that the only way of arriving at true knowledge is to tread the Path of Evil. But our system of White Magic teaches its pupils that only he who passes through the gate with clean life and pure heart can obtain his quest, and it is only with clean hands that he can lift the Grail.

You are told during the ceremony "to tread the pathway of Light," but that is barred, for it is impossible to live the entirely spiritual life in the flesh. The true path then is in the middle way; to live a true and upright life, not rejecting the Material plane.

This is not only the Gate through which we can pass, but there is always an elder brother waiting to help, which is one the functions of an elder brother. The word "priest" means "elder Brother" and one of his functions is to open the gateway; and we are told that we are all lay-priests and kings, all initiates must be ready to open to those that come after. Then the time will come when the Great elder brother will open the gates for us to meet HIM. That is the gate which David speaks of when he says "Lift up your heads O ye gates and the King of Glory shall come in." Thus shall we also be admitted to the Kingdom of God.

# B2

## *Lectures and Addresses*
## *for the 1=10 Grade*

1. Ancient Egyptian Religion (by M.C.)
2. How to Read the Scriptures (by M.C.)
3. The 12 Tribes and Their Relation to the Zodiac
   (by MacGregor Mathers)

# 1

# Ancient Egyptian Religion

*by M.C. (Mrs. Felkin)*

Of all the ancient religions, that of Egypt strictly concerns us. When the Hebrews went into Egypt, they were a small tribe with a strong family feeling; a clan, the Scotch would have called it. They were struggling towards the ideal of an over-ruling Providence who had set them apart from the rest of the world. They were nomads with little knowledge of learning beyond their skill in breeding cattle, but they had extraordinary tenacity and vitality and a well marked "Psychic" faculty. Two hundred years later they emerged a nation, wielded together by persecution, led by a man who had been trained in the Universities of the day, a man who could not only give the moral code which has proved to be the foundation of law and order ever since, but also a cosmological philosophy unsurpassed by any, and a sanitary and hygienic system which bears comparison with most modern.

Where did these leaders acquire their enlightenment? Moses was visionary, an idealist, but he was also an eminently practical man. He had been brought up at the Egyptian Court, trained in the college of the Egyptian priests, and by the age of forty he had passed all their severest tests and had become what is termed an Initiate. What is an initiate? Briefly, it is one who has passed beyond belief into a wider realm of knowledge. You believe what others tell you: you know only by intimate personal experience.

Thanks to the Egyptian habit of inscribing their history and doctrines on stone walls and parchment scrolls, we are now in a position to study a great deal of this "wisdom of the Egyptians" in which Moses was learned. Not all of it, however, for we know that the highest degree of teachings was always given orally, but enough remains to show us an extraordinarily profound and comprehensive religion and philosophy. All religions have two sides, the exterior which appeals to the majority, and the interior which is grasped by the few only, and this characteristic is strongly present among the Egyptians. For the majority there were many Gods under various forms and appellations; for the few there was the One, Eternal, Incomprehensible, manifesting in the threefold aspect of Father, Mother and Child.

Before we go further, I want you for a moment to consider the geographical position of Egypt. If you look at a map of the northern part of Africa you will see the Nile rising above the mountains and flowing northwards to the Delta. Along its shores is a strip of wonderfully fertile land, irrigated naturally by the annual rise of the waters, owing to conditions in the far off mountains: beyond that fertile strip lies the desert. That long narrow strip of irrigated land is Egypt. It has two great divisions, North and South, which in early times had separate kings: later on they were joined and Pharaoh received the title of King of the North and South and assumed the double crown with which frescoes and statues have made us familiar. But besides the two great divisions there were innumerable lesser ones called by names which correspond roughly to our countries. Each had its own capital, its own temple, and its own governor: more so, each one had its own peculiarly sacred animal which was preserved in the temple precincts, considered strictly "tapu"* by the inhabitants and mummified after death. It does not follow that the animal in itself was regarded as divine, but it was certainly considered symbolic of some attribute of divinity. Let us take for instance the animal with which we are all familiar, the cat. What are the peculiar qualities that the cat shares with its bigger cousins, the lion and the leopard? Remember that both these animals abounded in the deserts abutting Egypt. The Egyptian cat was, and is, a big, fierce, many coloured creature: its colour blends in with the desert and suggests the burning heat, the destructive force of the sun: it was a beast of prey, impossible, insatiate. So on one hand it typified all the forces of Fate, Visham or Karma. But the cat has other marked characteristics: physically it has the curious faculty of seeing in the dark: the pupils of its eyes contract to mere slits at noonday or in strong light; they expand to the whole width of the iris at night or in darkness. Therefore its eyes symbolise the moon which waxes and wanes. Moreover the cat is pro-life and a devoted mother: she will face any danger in the defence of her kittens, and she is also capable of great friendship with and devotion to human beings. So in this aspect she symbolises maternity, protection, womanhood. Under the one aspect she was dedicated to the lion-headed Goddess Sekhah, and under the other to Pasht, the Mother. The Temple of Bubastis was her special home and there innumerable tame cats were kept and regarded as sacred. It was a crime to kill one of them and when they died they were mummified and given all funeral honours.

So it was with each home: each had its own sacred animal, but in the process of time some of these animals were established as sacred throughout the whole kingdom. The hippopotamus and the vulture, like the cat, symbolise maternity. The ram and the bull represent the male principle and the scarabaeus beetle was sacred to the creator of the world. This gives us a curious little sidelight on the extent and the accuracy of the sci-

*This is a Maori word which is analogous to "taboo."

entific knowledge amongst the priests. The scarabaeus has the peculiar habit of laying its eggs in suitable material which it then rolls into pellets about the size and shape of a pea. Then it proceeds to roll along, pushing them with its head, assisted by its front legs, and using it hind to walk with. The pellet was taken as a symbol of the world, but a symbol must resemble that which it symbolises, and therefore it become evident that these ancient Egyptians knew that the world was round, not flat. Naturally enough the uneducated people identify the sacred animals with those Gods whom they were associated with, and as Egypt was invaded and conquered repeatedly by successive warriors who all brought their own Gods, which were added to those already accepted, there accumulated an enormous Pantheon: but Egypt had a characteristic in common with Britain: however varied her conquerors, they were all absorbed into herself until they too became Egyptian. Each Pharaoh in turn found that the only way to govern the country was to accept its traditions and teachings. His sons were trained by the priests and became in due course head, not only of State, but also of the religion.

From the confusion of animal Gods we penetrate by degree to a remarkable clear and rational cosmic religion, the inner teachings which lay behind all the rest. First, and beyond all, was the Supreme, Unmanifested, Ineffable—Amoun. Today we retain this mysterious name in Amen, with which we conclude both prayer and praise. By His command both heaven and earth came forth into being, and from their union issued five Gods, Osiris, Isis, Set, Nephthys and Anubis. The first three correspond to the Hindu Trinity, Osiris the Creator, Isis the Preserver, Set the Destroyer. Of the remaining two, Nephthys represents the passive aspect of the Feminine, while Anubis is at once the guardian of the sanctity of the Gods and the guide who leads those who earnestly seek after divine things. No doubt some of you are familiar with the story of Osiris and Isis, but I will repeat it for those who have not heard it.

Osiris and Isis descended to earth to live as King and Queen over Egypt and to teach the people the peaceful arts of agriculture. They showed them how to cultivate their fertile land and how to grow crops, especially wheat, and how to irrigate. The country flourished and the people prospered under their beneficent rule: it was a Golden Age. But after a time Osiris set forth on a journey in order to teach these arts to other people, leaving Isis as regent during his absence. No sooner than he was safely gone than his brother Set came upon the scene. He avowed friendship with Isis and gathered a party of the nobles about him and awaited the return of Osiris. In the meantime he gave orders for the construction of an elaborate and very beautiful coffin; that is, the outer shell a mummy is laid in before being put in the great stone sarcophagus. You know that the Egyptians paid a great deal of attention to all that pertains to death: the Pharaohs and priestesses especially had very wonderful mausoleums and coffins prepared during their lifetimes, elaborately painted, recording the story of their lives on earth and also their progress after death. Set then, no doubt, had an exceptionally beautiful coffin made. When at length his brother returned, Set took a foremost part in the rejoicing and gave a great feat in his honour.

During the feast the new coffin was produced and Set offered it as a gift to whomsoever it would fit. One after the other laid down in it, but for each it was too big or too small, for it had been made from the measurements of Osiris. At last he in turn lay down in it and immediately Set and his confederates shut down the lid securely and poured boiling lead through the holes which had been pierced in it. So Osiris died and they set him adrift in the great river which carried him away until the coffin was caught in the branches of a tree which had been submerged by flood.

Meanwhile, Isis discovered Set's treachery, for he had seized the Kingdom and would have taken her also had she not fled. For a long time she wandered to and fro in search of her husband: it was her tears falling on the bosom of the Nile which caused it to rise in flood and thereby prevent the coffin from drifting out to sea.

At last, after many adventures, she found and recovered the

body of Osiris and carried it to a hiding place in the papyrus swamps. There by the power of her love she recalled Osiris to momentary life, and from that recall was afterwards born Horus. But Osiris again lay in her arms and Isis set forth to collect the oils and spices with which to embalm him. In her absence, Set found the body and this time he tore it asunder in fourteen pieces which he caused to be scattered over the whole country. So when Isis returned she had again to set forth on her tragic quest. In the process of time she found the fragments, and on each place hallowed by the fragments of a relic she had a temple built. When Horus was born, her sister Nephthys helped to nurse him and then he was brought up with great care and was trained so that in due time he might avenge his father's death. He met and challenged Set and they fought a great battle, but in the end Set escaped in the form of a crocodile.

Here we have an allegorical history of the human race shown forth. The descent of the Initiate, his teachings and illumination followed eagerly for a time. The powers of evil entice man from his allegiance: the death and disappearance of the Initiate rescued from oblivion by the devotion of love: the survival of Light and subsequent struggle between Light and Darkness.

The Egyptians believed in the resurrection in a dual sense. A man rose again upon the earth in his children, but his spirit passed on to a spiritual world. They believed in a personal judgement after death: each man must stand before the judgement seat of Osiris who reviewed his deeds and awarded his judgement. The part of the recording angel seems to have fallen to Anubis, who was also guardian of the Sanctuary. If a person failed to pass the required tests he was turned back and sent to the level of the beasts. If he were passed, then Isis and Nephthys led him past the judgement house and he became one of the company of Gods, he became "Osirified." He must pass through the region which corresponds to purgatory and thence he rose through the planes of Light. The spirit was represented in hieroglyphics and frescoes as a bird hovering with outstretched wings, ready to soar.

# 2

# Reading of the Scriptures

*by M.C. (Mrs. Felkin)*

In studying the great scriptures of the world, we very soon find that there are at least four ways in which they may be approached:

1. They may be taken literally at their face value—a method which we find was almost universally accepted in the 19th century as regards the Bible, when we find even in regard to translation, "verbal inspiration," the shibboleth of a considerable number of those who call themselves the educated classes.

2. There is the opposite extreme to this, the practice of regrading them more or less as a haphazard collection of folklore and stories suitable for children, of value to men chiefly as indications of persistence of traditions. The leaders of this school wasted a vast amount of energy who tried to prove that the books were not written by the men whose names they bore, or in trying to prove that the scriptures (we use the name to denote scared writings of all nations—the Vedas, Koran, the Egyptian Book of the Dead, Hebrew Scriptures and all the

myths of Scandinavia, Greece and elsewhere) are originally either totemistic or else purely nature allegories.

3. There is a small but conservative group of those who seek to give a purely spiritual interpretation, maintaining that there is no historical basis at all for the various stories and traditions enshrined in these books.

4. Lastly, there is the steadily increasing school of occultists, to which we ourselves belong.

To the true occultist there is always a material basis which contains the key to the spiritual truth. So that the occultists will believe that any scripture worthy of the name must be regarded from all these points of view if the reader is to penetrate to its real message. Since we are chiefly concerned with Hebrew Scriptures, to which we accorded par excellence the title of the Holy Bible, we will conform our attention to that.

The Bible, then, must be regarded in the first place as an historical record, dealing for the most part with the rise and preservation of a small Semitic race who possessed certain strongly marked characteristics. In the second place, this history is dealt with in such a manner that it contains an almost unbroken parallel with the great cosmic phenomena observed and recorded by those occultists who were the forerunners of modern science: and thirdly, these records contain within them the stupendous drama of the human soul. Take any point of the Bible, haphazard and, if you have eyes to see and a heart to understand, you will find therein the story of God's dealing with man—man as an individual or as a human race.

We as members of a Secret Order that has existed for centuries, have this advantage over most of those who seek to interpret this extraordinary document. We start out with a hypothesis that a secret tradition has existed from time immemorial; that is, has been preserved by means of Occult Orders such as our own, and much of its teaching has been handed on by oral tradition and conveyed by means of ceremonial.

We are taught that humanity is the child of union between

animal and spirit, that our bodies are the logical product of age-long evolution, which is recorded in the Book of Genesis, the Book of Beginnings. Bearing in mind that this is a condensed, but unintelligible account of evolution. What do we find? "In the beginning" it says there was a Divine Intelligence which the human brain can only vaguely conceive. The Qabbalists named it the "AIN SOPH AUR"—Limitless Light; another title is the "Negative Existence" or we can speak of "Potential Energy." This energy manifested in that form which Kelvin postulated as "vortices"—there was a movement, but without form. But movement produces form, and therefore in the course of Aeons worlds were born, and as further aeons passed by, these worlds became differentiated and clothed. Remember that to the occultist there is no such thing as death; matter may change its form, but is indestructible. More than that, a world is a living being, an entity with its own soul and intelligence. It must pass through a process of growth and development, analogous to the growth of a tree or of a human being. It is no mere form to say "The moving stars sang together and the Sons of God shouted for joy."

Translating the "evening and morning" of our English version to denote the geological period, you will find that the account given in Genesis does not differ in any essential form than that given by modern science. In the process of time, the human form was produced: all traditions agree that man was primarily androgynous. We may take it that the record so far brings us down to what is known as the Lemurian stage. The world was clothed and inhabited, but is was very much less solid than we know it. Then came the separation of the sexes and the subsequent awakening of desire with the resultant "Fall" and its accompaniment of physical conditions very much as they are today. Here we reach the Atlantean Epoch. Those who can read the Akashic Record* tell us that humanity reached a very high

---

*This is a record of all events of things that have happened and are about to happen. Some psychics refer to it as being like a library. The American psychic Edgar Cayce used to obtain many of his prophecies there. The Lemurian and Atlantean period are also discussed by Cayce in his tens of thousands of readings, at great depth.

degree of civilisation. Now turn to the story of the Flood, and other lines of tradition speak of a great flood also. It is clear that at some time or another there existed a country that linked Africa and America, that some great cataclysm destroyed the country and drove the inhabitants to take refuge in the surrounding lands, forming colonies in Egypt, Mexico, Chaldea, India, and Mongolia.* All these colonies possessed certain traditions in common and recorded them with similar symbols. In all cases we find that beings of a Higher Race continued to appear occasionally and to impart instruction which was preserved more or less intact. The Hebrews claimed that their founder ABRAM came from Chaldea, his name AB-RAM, or Father of Ram, indicates that he was an Initiate of a High degree, for we find the title of "father" associated with advanced grades of all schools. Moreover, he not only received direct teachings from the higher planes, but in obedience to it, he altered the whole mode of his life and set forth to found a new school, or Order as we say. Here we may pause for a moment to note a remarkable parallel in the story of all the great Initiates, Rama, Buddah, Moses, and our own Founder. At a certain stage in their own progress they were driven forth from their inherited surroundings to found a new Order, so was Mahomet, so today is Abdul Baha Abbas Effendi. It would seem that to preserve the life of the spirit it is essential from time to time to bring an upheaval, and transplantation must take place.

From the story of Abraham to the Apocalypse of St. John we have the history of Initiation. You may, as I have said, take it historically as containing the fragmentary record of a nation. You may find abundant evidence of cosmic myths and totemistic beginnings; it is easy to see, for instance, that the Ram was the totem of the ancient Hebrews and that it is therefore constantly referred to in these stories. Or you may say that the Sun passes

---

*See *Sacred Mysteries Among the Mayans and the Quiches* by Augustus le Plongeon, 1886; 1973 edition by Wizards Bookshelf. This book goes on to back up Mrs. Felkin's statements concerning common languages in America and Egypt.

into the Sign of Aries in the period of the substitution of the Ram for Iaasc and the destruction of the Golden Calf of Moses. And again, you may quite accurately say that the story of Abraham represents the awakening of the human soul to the recognition which is inevitably followed by the sacrifice, the recognition of a Divine Presence and a sacrifice, actual or potential, of all to the Supreme Claim. It is the fashion now to speak of Jehovah as a Tribal Deity, to contrast his teaching and claims with those of CHRIST: yet if you look below the surface you will find that there is a fundamental identity. CHRIST also said "He that loveth father or mother, or wife or child, more than Me is not worthy": at some time or another in our progress we are confronted with that choice.

I do not propose to enter into any detailed analysis of the Bible: you can easily select points here and there which support the contention that to be understood it should be regarded from these varying standpoints. Take, for instance, the story of Joseph and his Brethren. On the face of it the number of actors immediately suggests a solar interpretation, the 12 brethren being the 12 Signs of the Zodiac. But again if you bear in mind a singular suggestiveness in this story, remember that in an Order the pupil is the Son, the teacher is also the Father. It is quite possible that in many cases this relationship was material as well as mental, but if we regard the Sons of Israel as being members of an Occult Order we will further recognise the fact that Joseph's coat of many colours was the robe of office with which Israel invested him as his chosen successor. It is natural then that the older members of the Order should resent having this youth appointed as their future Chief: their resentment was not lessened, but increased, when he showed, by his visions, that he was entitled to that office. Again we come to the necessary isolation and transplanting which the initiate must undergo. Jacob in his youth had been sent into exile that he might undergo his probation; Joseph must go through the same experience. I do not wish to lay down a hard and fast rule: I do not suppose that everyone who enters upon the Path must pass through this phase, but it has certainly been my experience.

There are two other characters whom I would like you to consider from the Order point of view, David and Solomon. David is
pre-eminently the type of Seeker, eager, passionate, and impul-
sive. In modern language we would say that he had the artistic
temperament, and since he never learned to control his passions and impulses, so he never attained to the higher grades,
for it was not given to him to build the Temple. Solomon was
exactly the reverse: in his youth he chose the mystic path: he
asked for and received the high grades of Chokmah and Binah.
In his arrogance he claimed that he need not undergo the pro-
bationary training: he need not lay the tiresome foundation in
the etheric* nor gain the victory over the astral. And so GOD
granted him the desire of his heart and sent leanness to his
soul. Having been allowed to build the Temple he yet failed to
dwell therein. To find the true Initiate of the Old Testament we
must turn to Elijah or to Isaiah. Elijah, I think, stands for the
ascetic: Isaiah for the mystic visionary, St. John the Baptist or
St. John the Divine.

This brings us to the New Testament, and I want you for a
moment to consider our everyday lives. I think that you will
find, broadly speaking, that life falls into two great divisions.
The small yet necessary incidents which occur but leave little or
no trace. They belong entirely to the material plane and have no
spiritual significance. But the other division belongs primarily
to the spiritual plane and is indeed a reflection of that which
exists externally. In reading the Gospels you will find that every
incident recorded bears this interior cosmic significance. Com-
mentators and critics may wrangle over the variations in the
accounts given and over the probable dates of the writings, but
those are details which concern us very little.

What does intimately concern us is that we have here the
record from out of four widely differing standpoints of One
Man's career. Try to realise that at the time when Jesus of
Nazareth was born, there were numberless Orders in existence,

---

*The Etheric Body or plane is next to the world as we now perceive it. The
Astral Plane is the next higher plane or level of existence.

the Essenes, the Parsees, the Nazarenes, and the Gnostics. All these were the veils more or less to Hidden Orders of which there is no direct record but which can be traced indirectly. It was from these Orders that the Apostles and the Outer Circle of Disciples were drawn. The common attribution of the Kerubic emblems to the four Evangelists gives us a clue to their respective Orders:—

| Matthew | Aquarius | Essene |
| Mark | Leo | Parsee |
| Luke | Taurus | Thearapeut |
| John | Scorpio (Eagle) | Gnostics |

Each of these was bound to have his outlook, memories and records, strongly coloured by his previous training, and yet how marvellously they agree in essentials.

I suppose most of you have wondered wherein Christianity differs from other great Wisdom religions. It is probably difficult for you to realise the attitude induced by the Calvinistic teachings which has made such a great profound influence on most Scotch and many English minds during the last three hundred years, though you partake of the subsequent rebound from that stern creed. The agnosticism of the 18th and 19th centuries was the inevitable revolt against the appalling doctrines of narrow minded ignorance which had striven to enslave men body and soul. Calvinism is in fact the counterpart of Islam, and in its logical position is that of a missionary with a Bible in one hand and a sword in the other. It was from this perversion of the teachings of Christ that the idea arose of GOD as an implacable Judge who could only be induced to pardon mankind from the everlasting punishment by the substituted punishment of a victim. This is not the teaching we find in the New Testament: what is?

You will remember in a previous lecture the diagram of the Principles on Man: I want you to observe that the attribution of Kether is Christos. Therein I think you will find the Key to the Inner Doctrines of Christianity, the doctrine which has been distorted and misunderstood in the exoteric churches. When the Great White Christ incarnated in the chosen vehicle of Jesus, whose body was a product of 42 generations of selection (note that 42=Beth, the House of Sacrifice), a stupendous cosmic event was consummated. The Divine Christ Principle, which had hitherto existed only potentially, now became the integral part of humanity. This is why we are told that after the Crucifixion (which is the symbolic perfection of the Union between Human and the Divine) CHRIST descended into Hell, he preached unto spirits in prison. Thenceforth it became possible for each human being to become a Christos or Chrestos (anointed or perfected). "I am the way" CHRIST tells us, and again. "I , if I be lifted up, will draw all men unto Me."

The Calvinists evolved the extraordinary doctrine of "imputed righteousness," which has been well likened to clothing a dirty man in a clean garment. The Scriptures tell us that "He shall save His people from their sins": He is truly the Saviour, but He saves us from our sins, not from their logical results. The CHRIST shows us the way to rise above sin, He teaches us the perfect Law of Love: we are to love GOD with the whole being and our fellow beings as ourselves, as brothers.

He sanctifies every form of Love: marriage becomes a sacrament and children GOD's messengers. Friendship is holy because He had friends; service is dignified because He had served others; "Love fulfilleth the Law." And from out of Love springs the true doctrine of vicarious suffering; for the strong may suffer in order to help the weak: the Path of Initiation is in its very nature the willing acceptance of suffering. The Initiate endures hardships, not merely that he may become purified himself, but rather that by his suffering he may help others who are not yet initiated and thus draw to them nearer to Union with GOD. As our master is the Atonement for matter, uniting in the consummation of his earthly life, Humanity with Divinity, so each of us is permitted to become in one degree part of the Atone-ment until all is consumed and becomes infinite and holy.

So we find that the New Testament is the logical sequence to the old. In the Old Testament we have a record of partial Initiation, the Way of the Glorified Adept, birth, suffering, endurance, vision, death, resurrection. And through all the consciousness of GOD in us, the Practice of the Presence of God.

*Note:* Two small Fishes = Light and darkness, Positive and negative, Male and Female. Five Loaves= Pentagram, Spirit and Four Elements, undivided Man. 5000 = Human Race, traditional period from Adam to Christ. 12 baskets = Divisions of the race, 12 Tribes, 12 Apostles, 12 Signs.

# 3

# The Twelve Tribes and Astrology

## by MacGregor Mathers

The Twelve Tribes* are thus attributed to the Twelve Zodiacal Signs and permutations of the Great and Holy Name of Tetragrammaton and the Angelic counterparts:

| Sign | Letters of the Name | Tribe | Angel |
|------|--------------------|-------|-------|
| Aries | Yod Heh Vau Heh | Gad | Melchidael |
| Taurus | Yod Heh Heh Vau | Ephraim | Asmodel |
| Gemini | Yod Vau Heh Heh | Manasseh | Ambriel |
| Cancer | Heh Vau Heh Yod | Issachar | Muriel |
| Leo | Heh Vau Yod Heh | Judah | Verchiel |
| Virgo | Heh Heh Vau Yod | Naphthali | Hamaliel |

*This lecture by Mathers has two versions. The only difference between them is that the Enochian names are placed in front of each tribe in one version. The Golden Dawn gave this lecture out at the 4=7 Grade. At Whare Ra Temple, it was given out first at 4=7 for a very brief time, then later at 1=10. It was incorporated into the "B" papers, though no indication is given in the Whare Ra papers as to who wrote it.

| Libra | Vau Heh Yod Heh | Asshur | Zuriel |
| Scorpio | Vau Heh Yod Heh | Dan | Barchiel |
| Sagittarius | Vau Yod Heh Heh | Benjamin | Advachiel |
| Capricorn | Heh Yod Heh Vau | Zebulun | Hanael |
| Aquarius | Heh Yod Vau Heh | Reuben | Cambriel |
| Pisces | Heh Heh Yod Vau | Simeon | Amnitzel |

Of these, especially the Bull, the Lion, the Scorpion (but in good symbolism the Eagle) and the Man are to be noted as forming the Kerubic figures of Ezekiel and John. To these signs are allotted the tribes of Ephraim, Judah, Dan and Reuben, who, as we shall presently see, encamped towards the Cardinal Points around the Tabernacle of the Congregation, and as the leaders of the others. The signs of the Twins, the Fishes, and in a certain sense as a compounded figure,* the Centaur armed with a bow, are also called bi-corporate, or double-bodied Signs. To these refer Manasseh, Simeon and Benjamin. Manasseh was divided into two half tribes with separate possessions (being the only tribe thus divided), and thus answers to the equal division of the Sign of the Twins, Castor and Pollux, the Great Twin Brethren. Simeon and Levi are classed together, like the two Fishes in the Sign, but Levi is withdrawn later, to form as it were the binding and connecting link of the Tribes, as the priestly caste. Benjamin is the younger brother of Joseph, for Rachael had only these *two* sons, and is the only one of the sons of Jacob who at his birth was called by two names, for Rachel called him "Ben oni," but his father Benjamin, and in the sign of the two natures of Man and Horse are bound together in one symbol.

We shall find much light upon the connection between the Signs and the Tribes shown by the blessing of Jacob, and of Moses, from the former of which the Armorial bearings of the Twelve Tribes are derived.

Let us note that as in the Tribes Levi was withdrawn, and the

---

*For an in-depth study of these tribes, see "The Testament of the Twelve Patriarchs" in *Lost Books of the Bible & the Forgotten Books of Eden.* Also see Ethelbert Bullinger's *Witness to the Stars.*

two Tribes of Ephraim and Manasseh substituted for the simple one of Joseph, so in the New Testament, Judas is withdrawn from the number of the twelve Apostles and his place filled by another, Matthias, who was chosen by lot to fill his place.

The following is the order by birth, of the children of Jacob: Leah bore Reuben ♒, Simeon ♓, Levi, afterwards withdrawn, and Judah. Bilhah (Rachel's maid) bore Dan ♏ and Naphthali ♍. Zilpah (Leah's maid) bore Gad ♈ and Ashur ♎. Leah again bore Issachar ♋, Zebulun ♑ and Dinah (a daughter). Rachel bore Joseph, whose sons were Manasseh ♊ and Ephraim ♉, but died at the birth of Benjamin ♐, whom she wished to call Ben-oni.

In the Wilderness the Tabernacle was pitched in the midst, and immediately surrounding it were the tents of Levi. At a distance towards the four cardinal points were the standards of the Twelve Tribes erected thus:—

| | |
|---|---|
| East | Judah, Kerubic Sign of ♌ |
| | with Issachar ♋ and Zebulun ♑ |
| South | Reuben, Kerubic Sign of ♒ |
| | with Simeon ♓ and Gad ♈ |
| West | Ephraim, Kerubic Sign of ♉ |
| | with Manasseh ♊ and Benjamin ♐ |
| North | Dan, Kerubic Sign of ♏ (Eagle) |
| | with Asher ♎ and Naphtali ♍ |

[See also the diagram on the following page.]

Save for the Kerubic emblems, the arrangement seems at first very confused; but when we notice the Maternal Ancestors of the Tribes, this confusion disperses, and we notice that at the East are three tribes descended from Leah, viz. Judah, Issachar and Zebulon. Opposite to them, towards the West, three tribes descended from Rachel, viz. Ephraim, Manasseh and Benjamin. At the South are two descended from Leah and one descended from Zilpah, viz. Reuben, Simeon and Gad, and at the North, two descended from Bilhah and one descended from Zilpah, viz. Dan, Naphthali and Asher. Here two tribes descended from Zilpah, Gad and Asher, are the only ones separated, and placed in opposition to each other, for these are two signs of the Equinoxes.

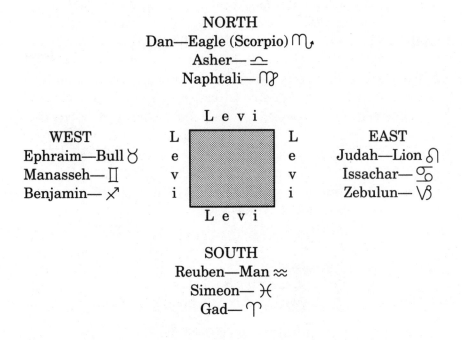

The substitution of the two tribes of Ephraim and Manasseh for the single one of Joseph is given in Genesis 48, where Jacob blessed them prior to the general blessing of the Tribes, stating at the same time that Ephraim, though the younger, should take precedence over Manasseh: "And Jacob said unto Joseph . . . And now thy two sons, Ephraim and Manasseh, which were born unto thee in the land of Egypt before I came unto thee in Egypt, are mine; as Reuben and Simeon they shall be mine. And thy issue which thou begettest after them shall be thine and shall be called after the name of their brethren in their inheritance . . . Morever I have given unto thee one portion above of thy brethren."*

Let us now notice the blessings of Jacob and Moses, and com-

---

*This is the Assyrian fish-god Oannes, who was half man and half fish.

pare them with the Signs of the Zodiac attributed to each Tribe. We shall take them in the Zodiacal order.

Of Gad (Aries), Jacob says, "Gad, a troop shall overcome him, but he shall overcome at the last." Moses says, "Blessed be he that enlargeth Gad: he dwelleth as a lioness, and teareth the arm with the crown of the head, and he provideth the first part for himself because there, in a portion of the law-giver, was he sealed; and he came with the heads of the people, he executed the justice of the Lord, and his judgements with Israel." The armorial bearings of Gad are, white, a troop of cavalry. All this coincides well with the martial and dominant nature of Aries, the only one of the twelve signs in which the superior planets alone bear sway, for it is the House of Mars, exaltation of the Sun and triplicity of Sun and Jupiter. The symbolism of the Lion is also proper to Aries on account of its solar, fiery and martial nature.

Of Ephraim and Manasseh (Taurus and Gemini), classed together under their father's name, Jacob says, "Joseph is a fruitful bough, even a fruitful bough by a well, whose branches run over the wall; the archers have surely grieved him and shot at him, and hated him: but his bow abode in strength, and the arms of his hands were made strong by the hands of the mighty God of Jacob; (from thence is the shepherd, the stone of Israel:) Even by the God of thy father, who shall help thee, and by the Almighty who shall bless thee with the blessings of Heaven above, blessings of the deep that lieth under, blessings of the breasts and of the womb: the blessings of thy father have prevailed above the blessings of my progenitors unto the utmost bound of the everlasting hills: they shall be on the head of Joseph, and on the crown of the head of him who was separate from his brethren." Moses says, "Blessed of the Lord be his land, for the precious things of heaven, for the dew, and for the deep that coucheth beneath, and for the precious fruits brought forth by the Sun, and for the precious things put forth by the moon, and for the chief things of the lasting hills. And for the precious things of the earth, and the fullness thereof, and for the good will of him that dwells in the bush: let the blessing come upon the head of Joseph, and upon the top of the head of him that was separate from his brethren. His glory is like the firstling of a bullock, and his horns are like the horns of unicorns: with them he shall push the people together to the ends of the earth, and they are the ten thousands of Manasseh.'

The Armorial Bearings of Ephraim are: Green, an Ox. Those of Mannesseh are flesh-colour, a Vine by a Wall. All this refers to the natures of Taurus and Gemini, the firstling of the bullock and the earthy nature of the sign, shown by the hills, to Taurus while the archers over Manasseh, as Sagittarius, the sign of the Archer, is in opposition to Gemini.

Of Issachar, Cancer, Jacob says: "Issachar is a strong ass couching down between two burdens: and he saw the rest was good, and the land that it was pleasant, and he bowed his shoulder to bear, and became a servant under tribute." Moses says: "Rejoice Issachar, in thy tents . . . and they shall suck of the abundance of the seas." The armorial bearings of Issachar are Blue, and an ass crouching beneath its burden. This coincides with the peaceful nature of the quiet and watery sign of Cancer.

Of Judah, Leo, Jacob says: "Judah, thou art he whom thy brethren shall praise: thy hand shall be in the neck of thine enemies; thy father's children shall bow down before thee. Judah is a lion's whelp: from the prey, my son, thou art gone up; he stooped down, he crouched as a lion, and as an old lion; who shall rouse him up? The sceptre shall not depart from Judah, nor a lawgiver from between his feet, until Shiloh come; and unto him shall the gathering of the people be. Binding his foal unto the vine, and his ass's colt unto the choice vine; he washed his garments in wine, and his clothes in the blood of grapes: his eyes shall be red with wine, and his teeth white with milk." Moses says, "This is the blessing of Judah, and he said, Hear, Lord, the voice of Judah, and bring him unto his people, let his hands be sufficient for him and be thou an help to him from his enemies." The armorial bearings of Judah are Scarlet, a lion rampant. All this well agrees with the regal and leonine nature of the Sign. "Binding the ass's colt unto the choice vine" may allude to the ass of Issachar, Cancer, lying between Judah, Leo, and the vine of Manasseh, Gemini.

Of Naphthali, Virgo, Jacob says, "Naphthali is a hind let loose, he giveth goodly words." Moses says, "O Naphtali satisfied with favour, and full with the blessings of the Lord, possess thou the West and the South." The armorial bearings of Naphthali are Blue, a hind.

Of Asher, Libra, Jacob says, "Out of Asher his bread shall be fat, and he shall yield royal dainties." Moses says, "Let Asher be blessed with children, let him be acceptable to his brethren, and let him dip his foot in oil. Thy shoes shall be iron and brass, and as thy days, so shall thy strength be." The armorial bearings of Asher are Purple, a Cup. All this coincides with the nature of Venus and Libra, while the feet refer to the sign of Pisces, which rules the feet, and in which Venus is exalted. Iron and Brass are the metals of the friendly planets of Mars and Venus.

Of Dan, Scorpio, Jacob says: "Dan shall judge his people as one of the tribes of Israel. Dan shall be a serpent by the way, and adder in the path, that biteth the horse's heels, so that his rider shall fall backward. I have waited for thy salvation, O Lord." Moses says. "Dan is a lion's whelp, he shall leap from Bashan." The armorial bearings of Dan are Green, an Eagle. These things fit with the martial and fierce nature of this sign in which Mars principally bears sway. To the sign of Scorpio, the Egyptians attributed the Serpent, and also Typhon, the Slayer of Osiris, and on this account they call it the "Accursed Sign." In good symbolism it is generally represented by the Eagle. The horse's heels which the Serpent sometimes bites are found in the Centaur figure of Sagittarius which follows Scorpio in the Zodiac.

Of Benjamin, Sagittarius, Jacob says, "Benjamin shall ravin as a wolf: in the morning he shall devour the prey, and at night he shall divide the spoil." Moses says: "The beloved of the Lord shall dwell in safety by him; and the Lord shall cover him all the day long, and he shall dwell between his shoulders." The armorial bearings of Benjamin are Green, a Wolf. These suit the character of Sagittarius, partly keen, partly of the nature of Jupiter, and partly brutal.

Of Zebulon, Capricorn, Jacob says: "Zebulon shall dwell at the haven of the sea, and he shall be for a haven of ships, and his border shall be unto Sidon." Moses says: "Rejoice Zebulon in thy going out, and Issachar in thy tents, they shall call the people unto the mountain, there they shall offer sacrifices of righteousness, for they shall suck of the abundance of the sea, of the treasures hid in the sands." This suits well the tropical, earthy and water signs of Capricorn and Cancer, The armorial bearings of Zebulon are Purple, a Ship.

Of Reuben, Aquarius, Jacob says: "Reuben, thou art my firstborn, my might, and the beginning of my strength, the excellency of dignity and the excellency of power. Unstable as water, thou shalt not excel, because thou wentest up to thy fathers bed, then defiledist thou it; he went up to my couch." Moses says: "Let Reuben live and not die, and let not his men be few." The armorial bearings of Reuben are Red, a Man. "Unstable as water" is still shown in the undulating hieroglyphic which marks this aerial and brilliant, but often superficial sign of the Water-Bearer.

Of Simeon and Levi, Pisces, Jacob says: "Simeon and Levi are brethren; instruments of cruelty are in their habitations. O my soul, come not thou into their secret, unto their assembly, mine honour, be not thou united: for in their anger they slew a man, and in their selfwill they digged down a wall. Cursed be their anger, for it was fierce; and their wrath, for it was cruel: I will divide them in Jacob, and scatter them in Israel." This alludes to their smiting Shalem, the city of Hamor and Shechem, and slaying the latter because they had carried off Dinah, the daughter of Leah. Moses says of them: "Let thy Thummim and thy Urim be with the Holy One, whom thou didst prove at Massah, and with whom thou didst strive at the water of Meribah; who said unto his father and mother, I have not seen him; neither did he acknowledge his brethren, nor knew his children; for they have observed thy word, and kept thy covenant. They shall teach Jacob thy judgements and Israel thy law: they shall put incense before thee, and whole burnt sacrifice upon thine altar. Bless, Lord, his substance, and accept the works of his hands; smite through the loins of them that rise against him, and of them that hate him, that they rise not again." The armorial bearings of Simeon are Yellow, a Sword.

These are the blessings of the twelve tribes of Israel, whose names were engraven upon the twelve stones of the High Priest's breastplate, upon which, according to some traditions, certain flashes of light appeared playing over certain of the letters, and thus returning the answer of the Deity to the consulter of the Oracle of the Urim.

By comparing these blessings with the nature of the Signs attributed to the particular tribes, we have thus been enabled to trace more or less clearly the connection between them, and also the derivation of the armorial bearings ascribed to them in Royal Arch Freemasonry.

# Daily Rhythm for the 1=10*

**On Rising:** 1=10 Sign and say—

"May the Fire of the Sun fill me with Life."

**Bath:** "May the purity of this water be mine."

**Dressing:** "Except Adonai build the house their labour is but lost who build it. Except Adonai keep the city, the watchmen waketh but in vain."

---

*I am unable to trace whether this was an original Golden Dawn document or something used only by the Stella Matutina or Whare Ra in particular. Personally, I find this "Rhythm" just a bit too Christianized for my taste, but for those who wish to use their own phrasing, it is an ideal way to become more aware of what grade you are working from. At Thoth Hermes, all those who go through this grade do the invoking pentagram of Earth in each quarter and then recite the prayer of the Gnomes from the ritual itself instead of using the "Daily Rhythm." The effect is quite stimulating when done every morning and evening, and it is every bit as effective as the "Daily Rhythm," if not more so. The same procedure is then carried out with each of the elemental grades.

**Noon:** "Let the earth Adore Adonai."

**Evening:** "Let the Earth Adore the Lord and King of the earth, Adonai, Adonai Ha-Aretz, Adonai Malekh. Blessed be Thy Name to the countless ages—Amen.

**Night:** "O Stability in Motion,
O Darkness veiled in Brilliance,
O day clothed in night,
O master who never doth withhold the wages of Thy workmen,
O silver whiteness,
O Golden Splendour,
O Crown of living and harmonious diamond,
May the blessing of Adonai be upon you all."

**Affirmations:** An easy way to gain strength during the day is by use of Affirmations. Such as:

"Praise the Lord O my Soul and all that is within me praise His Holy Name"

"All things are possible etc."

"He will give strength and power unto His people,
Let those who seek Thee be glad and joyful."

# The Elementals of the Earth Grade: The Gnomes*

We are all so accustomed to the presence around us of plants, trees, insects, reptiles, animals and birds that we take them for granted and do not realize how entirely alien their lives are from our own. They belong, in fact, to a different world from ours and their outlook must be from a different angle.

But when we are told there there are other living creatures not normally perceptible to our senses, we are apt to reject the idea as the survival of old fables and fairy tales. Nevertheless, such beings not only exist, but are of vital importance both to us personally and to the conduct of the world at large. Without their presence and unceasing activities the processes of life as we know it would cease to function. Let us examine this statement in some detail.

Where does life begin and how does it manifest itself?

---

*This is not a bad little paper, though unfortunately it does not go far enough. I do suggest the reader obtain a copy of the book *Devas and Men*, a compilation of work put out by the Theosophical Society, which goes into great detail on both elementals and devas. The structure of the elementals is an area that the Golden Dawn did not go into far enough.

Not so many decades ago we should have said that life begins with plants and manifests in movement. Now we have to realize that movement is to be found everywhere, in minerals, in metals, in earth, air, water and fire. So it seems profitable to think that there must be some form of life present in all the kingdoms of the world. Consider the Element of Earth for instance. Here we find the foundation of all the forms of life with which we are familiar. But if life springs from the earth then life must be inherent therein. Even in the great deserts of the world there is some form of life to be found, it may be in those curious plants which we class as cacti; it may be in the multifarious forms of insects and beetles. At the opposite extremes from these we have the teaming forests and swamps.

Both these extremes have one common requirement—that of movement—if the earth is to support life then it must be kept in constant movement; rocks must be broken up, soil must be crumbled and the various constituents of earth must be mingled in order to supply the necessary combination of the appropriate forms derived from it.

Now the expansion of these various movements rests in the hands of the gnomes. They are actually the living essences of the Earth and by their constant activity and unremitting attention they enable the Earth to nourish all other forms of life, directly or indirectly. In the old legends the Gnomes, Goblins, Pixies and Brownies are represented as guardians of treasure—as indeed they are. They guard the secret treasure house of life's origin and their unending task is to shift and blend in perpetual permutations. To form the veins of metal, the matrix of gems, they must call in the aid of the Fire Spirits, the Salamanders, so that together they may exert an inconceivable amount of pressure; for metals and gems are the product of the compression of certain ingredients. For the support of any form of plant life they must have the assistance of the Gnomes and Sylphs since a plant demands moisture and air to stimulate its growth. The Gnomes guard the activity of earth and roots, but the Sylphs must reserve and supervise the stems and leaves as soon as they appear above the ground.

Another thing that we find very hard to realize is that just as our eyes and ears can only discern a very small section of the immense scale of vibrations which build up the Universe, so also, our perceptions are usually aware of only those forms which approximate our own in vicinity. This applies to both ends of the spectrum. Our eyes cannot perceive the colors below dark crimson or above the delicate pinky-lilac which marks our boundaries, neither can our ears distinguish sounds below or above a certain range. In the same way we are normally unaware of forms which are either extremely dense or extremely tenuous, although such forms do exist and may, under given conditions, impinge upon our consciousness. We know from observation and experience that living creatures can move through those elements which are somewhat less dense than themselves, and that they must be formed to resist the external pressure of their own element. A fish moves with ease through the water, a bird through the air. Animals and man being denser than either of these require the support of earth to enable them to move easily in either water or air. But being more adaptable than fish or bird, man (and a few animals) can free himself to discard earth for a long period. Man can learn to swim, but if he is to fly he must have some support.

The Gnomes, and certain other entities with which we are not now concerned, live and move with ease through the earth. They are so dense that earth is to them as air is to us, and they move through it without consciously seeing it although they are aware of its varying degrees of density and the pressure exerted, just as we are aware of wind.

The human senses are not unlike stringed instruments which can be tuned in to a lower or a higher pitch. Therefore, it is possible so to tune in our perceptions that we become more or less clearly aware of these extra-normal living creatures. We know that the more any sense is trained, the more sensitive it becomes. A musician can distinguish notes to which an unmusical person is deaf; an artist perceives colors to which most of us are blind. And in the same way a trained occultist becomes aware of the infinite range of life which is in active existence all about us.

# Part 4

# The Ritual According to A. E. Waite

# The Ceremony of Advancement in the 1=10 Grade of Zelator

*Newly Constructed from the Cipher Manuscripts,
and Issued by the Authority of the Concealed Superiors
of the Second Order, to Members of Recognised Temples*

*A. E. Waite's Version of the Zelator Ritual
Privately Printed 1910*

## The Solemn Ceremony of Opening the Temple in the Grade of Zelator

The arrangement of the Temple is shown in the Official Diagram of the First Point.

If the Temple should not have been opened previously in the Grade of Neophyte, the ceremonial robing of Members and Officers, the clearing of the Temple and the Invocation at the Throne of the East are performed as exhibited therein. The Hierophant takes his place and assumes the Sceptre of his Office. The Members and Officers are seated, the position of the Zelatores being in the North-East of the Temple. The titles and duties of Officers are identical with those of the Neophyte Grade.

*Hierophant:* —〕—

All rise. The Sentinel leaves the Temple.

175

Hierophant: Fratres et Sorores *of the Holy and Glorious Order of the ∴ ∴, assist me to open the Temple with recollection and great reverence in the Grade of Zelator. Frater Kerux, I direct you to see that the Temple is guarded on the hither and further sides, remembering the Treasure that is within.*

The Kerux raises his Lamp and Wand in obeisance to the Hierophant, and passing to the door of the Temple knocks once on the hither side—ꓕ—. The Sentinel responds on the outer side, using the hilt of his Sword—ꓕ—. The Kerux turns to the East with uplifted Wand.

Kerux: *Truly Honoured Hierophant, I testify by the Pearl of Great Price that the Portal is watched and guarded.*

Hierophant: Fratres et Sorores, *let us see to the guarding of the sacred and beautiful Light which has come in the Morning Redness to hearts that are prepared within.*

This is said with raised eyes and uplifted Sceptre, and there follows a moment's pause.

Hierophant: *Honourable* Frater Hiereus, *I command you to prove the Brethren; assure yourself that all present have been advanced to the Grade of Zelator and are zealous students, seeking the Holy Ends.*

The Hiereus leaves his Throne, passes to the door of the Temple, where he draws his Sword and uplifts it.

Hiereus: Fratres et Sorores, *in the name of the Holy Watchers, and by the ordinance of the Truly Honoured Hierophant, I demand the Sign of the Grade.*

This being duly given, the Hiereus sheathes his Sword.

Hiereus: *Truly Honoured Hierophant, in obedience to your commands, I have received from the* Fratres et Sorores *the Sign of intervention and mediation, which is that of the Grade of Zelator.*

He communicates the Sign to the Hierophant, by whom it is

repeated in turn.

Hierophant: *I testify on my own part, and on behalf of the whole Order, that we who are present have been dedicated by our own free will, and have pledged and set apart ourselves, seeking the high things belonging to this Grade of Zeal. Interpose, O Lord, in Thy mercy, and so sustain those who have entered within the Gate that they may come at last to Thy Presence.*

This is said with raised eyes and uplifted Sceptre, and there follows a moment's pause.

Hierophant: *Let the Temple be hallowed with sacred fire, to symbolise that consecration of the earthly part of our nature which God fulfills within us.*

If the Temple has not been consecrated previously in the Neophyte Grade, the Dadouchos comes round with the sun to the Throne of the Hierophant, the blessing of the Vessel of Incense takes place in the prescribed form and the Dadouchos returns with the sun to his proper place. Then—and in either case—he advances to the Pillars and, standing between them, makes a Cross in the air with his Thurible and offers incense three times. He makes obeisance to the Hierophant between the Pillars and uplifts his Vessel.

Dadouches: *It is written that God shall save both man and beast. I have consecrated the Temple with Fire.*

He returns to his place.

Hierophant: *Let the Temple be cleansed with water, to symbolise the greater purification by which we are purified from stain in our earthly part.*

The same form of procedure is followed by the Stolistes, and when he passes between the Pillars he makes a Cross with his Aspergillus and sprinkles thrice. Thereafter he makes obeisance to the Hierophant and raises the Cup of Water.

Stolistes: *He that is washed, needeth not save to wash his feet, but is clean every whit. I have purified the Temple with water.*

He retires to his place. The Kerux comes forward and, standing between the Pillars, lifts up his Lamp and Wand, saying:

Kerux: *The body of the Temple is cleansed.*

Hierophant: *But I testify that there is another Temple, which is the body of man and his actions. Do Thou cleanse, O Lord, our earthly part, and bring us to see Thy face.*

This is said with raised eyes and uplifted Sceptre, and there is a moment's pause.

Hierophant: *Let us name the Element to which this Grade is attributed, that the sense of its dedication may be awakened, O Honourable* Hegemon, *in the hearts of those who are here and now present and in the uplifted heart of the Order.*

Hegemon: *It is the Grade of the Element of Earth and the material of the work of the wise. The earth is the Lord's and His is the fullness thereof.*

Hierophant—ı—: *Now, therefore,* Fratres et Sorores, *let us offer up our souls in adoration, giving glory and thanks and honour to the Lord and King of Earth.*

The Hierophant descends from his Throne and faces the East in front of it.

Hierophant (with upraised Sceptre in the sign of the 1=10 Grade): Adonai Ha Aretz, Adonai Malkah (he makes the Kabalistic sign of the ✠), *unto Thee be the Kingdom, the Power and the Glory,* Malkuth, Geburah *and* Gedulah, *the Valley of Vision, the Seat of Judgment and the Place of Magnificence: unto Thee be the Rose of Sharon, the Lily of the Valley, the indwelling glory and fountain of all influx, wherewith the Garden is watered for ever and ever.*

This Sign of the Grade is given by all present. The Kerux proceeds to the North and sprinkles Salt before the Tablet of the North, saying:

Kerux: *Amen. Let the earth adore* Adonai.

He returns to his place. The Hierophant faces West, standing in front of his Throne, and says with raised eyes and uplifted Sceptre:

Hierophant: *And purified, consecrated, dedicated, let the part of earth of his servants, the holy body of man, adore* Adonai.

He proceeds by South around the Altar to the Northern part of the Temple and there as he pauses:

Hierophant: *For the body is a holy sanctuary and the Lord is the light therein. Wherefore we look for its adoption, to wit, the redemption of the body, that it may be the body of heaven in its clearness.*

The Hierophant stands facing the Tablet of the North, at a convenient distance, say, six feet therefrom. The Hiereus, coming up by the North, takes his place at the right of the Hierophant, and the Hegemon is on his left side. The Stolistes stands behind the Hiereus and the Dadouchos behind the Hegemon. All Officers and Members face North.

Hierophant: *From the Palace at the Centre, the Sublime Palace, wherein is the King in His Beauty, to the Palace of Material Things, wherein reigns the Lord of the visible world in the likeness of the Lord of Glory, the order and sequence of high and holy mysteries proceeds without break or interruption, and man aspires to the Eternal in the height and depths of his nature. In the mystic name* Adam, *the letter* Aleph *looketh towards the Supreme Crown; the letter* Mem *looketh towards the Great Mother in* Binah, *who is the Divine Mother of souls; but the letter* Daleth *looketh towards the Sephira Malkuth and the mother in manifestation. May the grace of the Lord descend upon me and the brightness of the*

*Lord encompass me, while I recite the Sacred Invocations.*

The Hierophant lifts up his Sceptre.

Hierophant: *It was said of old by the* Elohim: *Let us make* Adam *in our image, after our likeness—the things which are manifest after the mode of things that are unmanifest and the will below in correspondence with the will which is above. It was said also: Let them have dominion over the fish of the sea and the lower emotions which they symbolise; over the fowl of the air, which are the wandering thoughts of the mind; and over the cattle and over all the earth—over every material part—and over every creeping thing that creepeth upon the face of the earth. And the Elohim created* Eth-Ha-Adam, *which is the Archetypal Man, as the pattern of the natural man; in the image of the* Elohim *created they him, male and female created they them.*

The Hierophant makes a great circle in the air concentric with the Tablet of the North. Therein he makes the Invoking Pentagram of Earth, saying:—

Hierophant: *Sanctify our congregation, O Lord; clothe us with the garment of salvation; cover us with the robe of righteousness, as a bridegroom is adorned with jewels. In the name of* Adonai Malkah, *the Bride and Queen of the Kingdom, looking towards the Gates of Light, Spirits of Earth, adore* Adonai.

He hands his Sceptre to the Hiereus, takes the Sword of the Hiereus, and makes the Sign of the Ox therewith in the centre of the Pentagram, saying:—

Hierophant: *In the Name of* Auriel, *the Great Angel of Earth, Leader of Heavenly Hosts, in memory of the manifested Law, and by the sign of the Head of the Ox, Spirits of Earth, adore* Adonai.

Returning the Sword to the Hiereus, he takes the mitre-headed Sceptre of the Hegemon and makes a Cross in the air, saying:—

Hierophant: *By the sacred Names and Letters which are inscribed on the Tablet of Earth, and by the inward mystery which they communicate, Spirits of Earth, adore* Adonai.

Returning the Sceptre to the Hegemon, he takes the Cup of the Stolistes and, making a ✠, sprinkles thrice in the North, saying:—

Hierophant: *By* Emor Dial Hectega, *the Divine Names which are written about the Northern Quarter of the Universe, by the protection from the enemy therein, and by their grace operating in man, Spirits of Earth, adore* Adonai.

Returning the Cup to the Stolistes, he takes the Thurible from the Dadouchos and, making a ✠, offers incense, saying:—

Hierophant: *By* Ic-Zod-He-Chal, *the Sacred Name attributed to the Symbolic King of the North, Spirits of Earth, adore* Adonai.

Returning the Censer to the Dadouchos, he receives his Sceptre from the Hiereus, and goes back to his Throne in the East. The other Officers also return to their places. All members face as usual.

Hierophant (with raised face and uplifted Sceptre): *Seal us, O Lord, for ever with Thy Holy Names; may they be written about the hearts of Thy servants.* Fratres et Sorores, *the Spirit and the Bride say, Come; and come therefore, my Brethren: bring offerings of aspiration and come into the House of the Lord. In the Name of* Adonai Malkah, *the House is swept and garnished; the Temple is duly opened in the Holy Grade of Zelator.*—ﾠﾠ—

The Battery is repeated by the Hiereus and Hegemon. The Sentinel re-enters the Temple. Officers and Members are seated.

Here ends the Solemn Ceremony of Opening the Temple in the Grade of Zelator.

## The Ceremonial Advancement of a Neophyte to the 1=10 Grade of Zelator

### The First Point

The Hegemon is seated at the eastern side of the Altar, facing West. The Throne of the Hierophant has been placed on the southern and that of the Hiereus on the northern side of the Altar, both facing West. The Kerux, Stolistes and Dadouchos occupy a parallel line behind the Pillars and looking towards the East.

Hierophant: Fratres et Sorores, *the dispensation of the High Light has been committed to our charge, working towards the will in its conversion under the mystery of the Divine Will; and seeing that from the Unknown Superiors, who communicate the gifts of compassion behind the order of the ∴ ∴, I have received a warrant for its exercise in the person of our beloved Frater,* Adveniat Regnum (vel alius), *a Neophyte of this Holy Order, and am empowered duly to promote him from the Portal of the ∴ ∴.. I beseech you to unite with me spiritually in the consecration of his natural body for the better manifestation, the greater preparation and liberation of the man within. Do you therefore, Honourable* Frater Hegemon, *our Mediator and Reconciler, Prince of Purity and Lord of Peace, go forth and prepare the Candidate, in the grace and the light, the benediction and mystic beauty, of your all-saving office.*

The Hegemon rises, makes obeisance with the Sign of the grade and leaves the Temple by South and West.

Hierophant: *Fratres et Sorores, the Neophyte is prepared in the body because already he is prepared in the mind; he holds the outward warrants of advancement, being warranted from within the Order, seeing that we are acquainted with his zeal. The light is not hidden which he received in the Portal of the ... ..... I pray you to prepare for him a place in your own hearts, that the love of brotherhood may encompass him who is on the Quest of Divine Love. Concur with me also in his advancement, that with recollection and reverence we may lead him beyond the gate and place him at the entrance of that symbolic path which leads to the Hidden Wisdom.*

The Hegemon has in the meantime prepared the Neophyte, who wears the Ribbon of his Grade, is hoodwinked and carries the Fylfot Cross in his right hand. The Hegemon instructs him in the battery proper to the Grade. When it has been given by the Neophyte, the Kerux turns down the lights and opens the door, so that it is just ajar.

Hegemon (speaking for Candidate): *Let me enter the Gate of Wisdom, for without are darkness and sorrow, and the eye opens in vein.*

The Kerux throws back the door and admits them. It is closed by the Sentinel.

Kerux: *May that which has opened at your knocking be even as the House of God and to you as the Gate of Heaven.*

Hegemon (for Candidate): *Open to me the gates of righteousness; I will go into them; I will praise the Lord.*

Kerux: *Come in peace. The Lord loveth the Gates of Zion more than all the dwellings of Jacob.*

The Hegemon advances slowly with the Candidate, and pauses at the speech of the Hierophant.

Hierophant: *The beginning of wisdom is the most true desire of discipline, and the care of discipline is love, and love is the keeping of her laws; and the keeping of her laws is the firm foundation of incorruption; and incorruption bringeth near to God. Therefore the desire of wisdom bringeth to the everlasting kingdom.*

Hegemon: *I have passed through the gates of understanding; I have come to the gate of wisdom; I have passed the threshold thereof: O give unto me the path of peace, the path which leads to the Temple and the place where wisdom dwells. I will build my tabernacle thereby and abide in the light of her presence.*

Hierophant: *Except the Lord build the House, they labour in vain that build it; except the Lord keep the city, the watchman waketh but in vain. May He keep your city for ever, O Neophyte of the ∴ ∴.. May He build your house in beauty. By what aid have you come to our Portal? Who has brought you across the threshold? Who leads you on this holy ground?*

Hegemon: *The call has come to the Wardens, and by a gracious act of intervention they have decreed the advancement of this our beloved* Frater. *The call is dual and the call is also one; it is from the depths of the heart of the aspirant and from that which is withdrawn in the Order—a sacred motive working in goodwill towards man. The Neophyte therefore enters by an act of permission and an act on his own part. The aids to entrance are in the sense of this dual motive. It is written that the earth is the Lord's and the fullness thereof; the Neophyte is guided by* Adonai, *the Lord of the earth. He is qualified by the knowledge that there is a secret path of wisdom; he is recognised by the dispensation, which you hold; the secrets of the 0=0 Grade are treasured in his heart; and he carries the Hermetic Cross.*

The Hegemon takes the Symbol, exalts it in the sight of the Hierophant, and it is then given to the Kerux.

Hierophant: Frater Kerux, *I direct you to receive from the Neophyte the Step, Sign, Token, Grand-Word and temporal Pass-Word communicated at the last Equinox.*

This is done accordingly, the Candidate being prompted when necessary and assisted throughout by the Honourable Frater Hegemon, with fraternal and loving care. Having received the Pass-Word, the Kerux faces the Hierophant, giving the salute of the Grade, and says:—

Kerux: *Truly Honoured Hierophant, I have received the secrets of the Neophyte Grade.*

Hierophant: *They are the outward forms of our mysteries; let us remember that the body of our sacred Ritual is not not without its spirit. . . .* Frater Hegemon, *you will lead the Neophyte to the due West of the Temple, and place him between the Pillars, with his face toward the East.*

This is done is due form, the Hegemon leading the Candidate.

Hierophant: Frater Adveniat Regnum (vel alius), *he who certifies that God is his aid, when he enters our Holy Temple, will ever command our own. Stand therefore,* Frater, *and, erect between the mystic Pillars, bear witness to your high intention. Do you covenant to maintain the same honourable and perfect silence regarding the Mysteries of this Grade which you have already been pledged to preserve respecting those belonging to the Portal of the ∴ ∴? Will you never reveal them to the world? Will you never confer them on a Neophyte, except by dispensation from the Second Order? And do you testify with true lips, in the presence of the brethren who are here and now assembled, that the dispositions that brought you to the Portal have passed into a sense of dedication, and that you will continue to the best of your ability to be worthy of your high calling?*

The Neophyte (being prompted by the Hegemon and repeating the words after him): *I pledge my soul to silence; I will communicate only as I have received in the ceremonies of the Temple, and the sense of my dedication burns like a holy fire in my heart.*

Hierophant: *I now bid you kneel down, place your right hand upon the earth, and as one who calls upon his proper body in testimony, say in a clear voice: I give my body to the gods; I will go where the great gods are: I swear by the earth whereon I kneel and by the body with its activities and all the train of their consequences. Let me be uplifted from the earth; let me tread the wine-press of the Kingdom.*

This is repeated by the Neophyte, following the Hierophant.

Hierophant: *And even as the immemorial soul, may your heart continue to demand the higher things.* Honourable Frater Hegemon, *in virtue of the sacred testimony which has been borne on his knees by the Candidate, let him be restored to the light.*

The Hegemon unbinds the eyes of the Candidate and the Kerux turns up the lights. The Hegemon repairs to his proper place and the Neophyte remains kneeling between the Pillars, his hand still upon the ground. The Kerux goes to the North, takes the vessel of Salt from the pedestal of the Tablet of the North, and, passing with the sun round the Altar, presents the vessel to the Neophyte.

Hierophant: Frater Adveniat Regnum (vel alius), *the seekers of eternal life are the salt of the earth. Take salt in your left hand, cast it towards the North and say in remembrance of your covenant: Let the mystical powers of earth bear witness to this my pledge.*

This is done accordingly.

Hierophant: *Rise therefore, O Neophyte, an accepted Postulant for advancement to the Grade of Zelator.*

The Kerux, having assisted the Neophyte, replaces the Salt and returns with the sun to his seat.

Hierophant: *With Water from the Wells of Understanding do Thou cleanse us, O Lord, from sin; with Fire from the Altar of Incense, do Thou consecrate us again to Thy service, that we may offer up a clean sacrifice in Thy Holy Place.* Fratres Stolistes et Dadouchos, *approach in the grace and sanctification of your respective offices; purify the earthly part of our beloved Postulant.*

The Stolistes comes round the Pillars, holds up his Vessel of

Water in obeisance to the Hierophant, turns westward, cross-marks the Neophyte on the forehead and sprinkles three times before him, saying:

Stolistes: *Waters of purification, Waters of the Great Sea, for the cleansing of the earth and man, I purify with water.*

He turns eastward, again elevates his Cup before the Hierophant, and returns to his seat. The Dadouchos comes round the Pillars, holds up the Thurible in obeisance to the Hierophant, turns westward, raises his Thurible before the Candidate, makes the sign of the Cross therewith and censes him thrice, saying:

Dadouchos: *Fire from the Altar which is above; Fire for the consecration of earth and man: I consecrate with fire.*

He turns eastward, again elevates the Thurible before the Hierophant and goes back to his seat.

Hierophant: *The blessing of the Order overshadows you, its welcome awaits you, its God-speed goes before you, as you pass from the gates of the Temple towards the Sanctuary that is within. You have knelt between the Pillars, to lay down the uneasy yoke and the intolerable burden of the old unconsecrated life; you have arisen between the Pillars to the new and dedicated life. Between the Pillars you have been purified and made ready in the sense of the life of dedication; its vistas stretch before you. You stood in the Portal of the ∴ ∴ at the threshold of our discipline. I bid you lift up the eyes of your spirit, for this is holy ground, and that which lies before you is the path of your attainment and return. Hail unto you, our Postulant and* Frater, *for your blessed dispositions towards the Light.*

   *And* Tetragrammaton Elohim *planted a Garden eastward in Eden; and there He put the man whom He had formed. And out of the ground made* Tetragrammaton Elohim *to grow every tree that is pleasant to the sight and good for food: the Tree of Life also in the midst of the Garden, and the Tree of Knowledge of Good and of Evil. And a river went out of Eden to water the Garden, and from thence it was parted and became into four heads. The Tree of Knowledge of Good and of Evil in in the* Sephira Malkuth, *which is also the inferior Garden, wherein are good and evil. For in the correspondence of things which are above with those that are manifested below, there is a Supernal and there is a Lower Eden. The one is the place of our desire and the place whence the influx cometh; the other is that of our purgation. From* Gedulah, *or* Mercy, *there is derived into* Malkuth *the influx of benignity and mildness, on the side of goodness, and from* Geburah *an influx of severity, on the side of evil. The good therein is called the Archangel* Metatron *and the evil is the Archangel* Samael. *It is the Tree of divided Knowledge and it shall be united with the Supernal in* Daath. *But the Tree of Life which stood in the midst of the Garden is that Tree by which* Malkuth *is united with* Binah. *Herein is a great mystery. For the way of the Tree of Life is by the way of Knowledge, and the union with the Supernal in* Daath *is by the middle path which is kept by the Archangel* Sandalphon. *But this allegory of* Malkuth *is also in the mystical sense an allegory of the body of man, above which there is the crown of all life. It is said of the middle path that above it are the Blessed Souls and the Holy Angels, but the* Kliphoth *or demons dwell beneath its roots. So also the permanent part of our nature is above and the shells of wandering thoughts and evil dreams are below.*

The Hegemon rises in his place, with uplifted Sceptre.

Hegemon: *Guide us, O Lord, and guard in all our ways. Let the Neophyte enter the path of Evil.*

The Kerux, with Lamp and Wand, leads the Postulant by the North-East towards the Hiereus, who rises with drawn Sword to meet them.

Hiereus: *Whence come you?*

Kerux (answering for Neophyte): *I come from between the mystic Pillars; I seek the way to the heights and the Path of Life in the Name of* Adonai.

Hiereus: *I am* Samael, *the Great Angel, the Prince of Darkness and of Evil. I am the providence of God in its concealment, trying and sifting the elect, but not beyond their strength. You have called upon the Name of the Lord; return in that Name of majesty: you shall not pass by.*

The Kerux leads back the Neophyte by the same way, that is to say, against the sun, and sets him between the Pillars. The Hegemon rises in his place, with uplifted Sceptre.

Hegemon: *Watch us, going forth and returning; watch us, O Lord, for ever. Let the Neophyte enter the path of Goodness.*

The Kerux leads the Postulant by the South-East and brings him before the Hierophant, who rises with uplifted Sceptre.

Hierophant: *Whence come you?*

Kerux (answering for Neophyte): *I come from between the mystic Pillars; I seek the way to the heights and the Path of Life in the Name of* Adonai.

Hierophant: *I am* Metatron, *the Great Angel—Angel of the Divine Presence and Indwelling Glory, the Legate of* Shekinah. *It is not in the law and the order to overleap every thing and attain perfection at once. Your eyes cannot stand its brightness. Return in the Name of the Lord: your time is not yet, and you can not pass by.*

The Neophyte is led back by the Kerux to his place between the Pillars. The Hegemon rises for the third time with uplifted Sceptre.

Hegemon: *Lead us, O Lord, until our death, that we may come alive into Thy Presence. Let the Neophyte enter the strait path, as one of the few that find it. It turneth not to the right or to the left. I have watched long for your coming, O Son of*

*Truth.*

The Kerux leads the Neophyte up the centre of the Temple and halts at the Western side of the Altar. The Hierophant and Hiereus rise together and turning inward join their Sceptre and Sword over the Altar, saying together:—

Hierophant
Hiereus } : *Whence come you?*

Kerux (for Neophyte): *I come from between the mystic Pillars; I seek the way to the heights and the Path of Life, in the name of* Adonai.

The Hegemon rises and between the Sceptre of the Hierophant and the Sword of the Hiereus he thrusts his own mitre-headed Sceptre, raising it to an angle of * *. He thus parts them asunder with the Sign of the Grade.

Hegemon: *I am* Sandalphon, *the Great Angel; I am the left-hand, feminine Kerub of the Ark, as the Hierophant is the male Kerub on the right hand. I rise in the place of Benignity. I come from before the Golden Mercy-Seat. I am the Preparer of the Way which leads to the Celestial Light. Peace and reconciliation are in my hands. I have the power and will to save all who shall enter by the middle path of prudence. I have seen the Tree of Life and the twelve manners of fruit. Make way for me, ye Lords of Truth; I carry the grace of mediation, and before I have finished my course I look to make all things one.*

The Hierophant and Hiereus resume their seats South and North of the Altar respectively. The Hegemon remains standing.

Hegemon: *And* Tetragrammaton Elohim *placed at the East of Eden* Kerubim *and a Flaming Sword, which turned every way to keep the way of the Tree of Life.* Frater Adveniat

Regnum (vel alius), *from* Malkuth, *which is the tenth* Sephira, *the manifested world, the incorporation of man's spirit in flesh, there extends a middle path, and it is the way of your return to the height. It is the path of Equilibrium between the Evil and the Good, and at some far point thereof the Tree of Knowledge shall become the Tree of Life. We have told you concerning that Tree in the middle of the mystic Garden, of the original condition of man when the Divine Substance was continually communicated to his soul. You know that he was sent forth into exile and since that strange prenatal time has been the denizen of an inferior garden. But the vestiges of the old transcendent state have not been removed utterly. The scattered fragments of the Divine Food allure him still in his exile; they are administered in the sacraments of Nature and Grace for ever and ever; they are the aids and consolations accorded to him in the way of his return homeward; they are the sanctities of the path of his redemption. Remember therefore, O Frater, whence you have come; remember whither you are going: lift up your eyes and know that salvation is continually at hand.*

The Hegemon resumes his seat. The Hierophant rises to confer the secrets of the Grade as follows:

Hierophant: *Receive now the official secrets which are reserved to the Grade of* Zelator. *They consist of a Step, Sign, Grip or Token, a Word, a Mystic Number and a Pass-Word formed therefrom. The Step is taken \* \* \* \*. It indicates that you have crossed the Threshold. In this position extend \* \* \* \*. This is the Sign of the Grade, and it commemorates the manner in which the* Hegemon *interposed for your assistance between the Hierophant and* Hiereus, *acting as guardians of the paths. The Grip or Token is exchanged by \* \* \* \*. This is the distinguishing grip of the First Order. The Word is \* \* \*, signifying \* \* \* \*, and refers to the Queen of the Earth, to which element this Grade is attributed. The Mystic Number is \* \* \*, and from it is formed the Pass-*

*Word * * *, meaning Ornament. It is to be lettered separately when given. The Badge of this Grade is the Ribbon of the Neophyte, with the addition of a Red Cross within the triangle, and the numbers 1 and 10, within a circle and a square respectively, left and right of the apex of the triangle.*

The Hierophant invests the Neophyte with the Ribbon and continues:

Hierophant: *The three Portals in the East are the Gates of the Paths leading to three further Grades which with those of* Zelator *and* Neophyte *constitute the first and lowest circle of our Fraternity. They also represent the Paths which connect the* Sephira Malkuth *with the* Sephiroth *which are above. The Portals are inscribed in their centres with the Hebrew letters,* Tau, Quoph *and* Shin, *being the consonants of the mysterious word* Quesheth, *which signifies a bow. It is a reflection in things beneath of that rainbow which is said, in another form of symbolism, to encircle the Throne of God. It refers also to the Quest of the Self-Knowing Spirit in the path of manifestation and to the Eternal Covenant between the Divine in man and the Divine in the Universe by which there is, world without end, a path of return to God.*

The Hierophant resumes his seat. The Hegemon rises in his place and comes round to the West of the Altar.

Hegemon: *The Flaming Sword of the* Kerubim *is represented by the most simple outline of its symbolism in the diagram before you. It has however a much deeper meaning than that of the symbolic weapon which kept the way of the Tree of Life.* Frater Adveniat Regnum (vel alius), *may God be with you in your Quest, and seeing whence you have come down, may His own wisdom teach you the most practical of all lessons—which is how to go back.*

The Hegemon returns to his place. The Hiereus rises from his seat and faces towards the Altar.

Hiereus: *In the Grade of Neophyte the Red Cross was placed at the apex of the White Triangle upon the Altar, but is placed within it in this Grade, to symbolise the Divine Life abiding in the Divine Light. When the Light of the Spirit is declared, my Brother, in your consciousness, may the Life be communicated to you therein.*

He resumes his seat. The Hierophant rises in his place to indicate the Tablet of the North.

Hierophant: *The Grade of Zelator is referred in our mystical symbolism to the element of earth, and one of its emblems is called the Tablet of Earth, the Northern Quadrangle and the Great Watchtower of the North. It is one of the four Elemental Tablets said to have been entrusted by the Holy Angel Avé to that patriarch Enoch who walked on earth with God, until a day came when he was not, for God took him. The Tablet contains Divine and Angelical Names referable in symbolism to the Northern Quarter of the heaven and by correspondence to the element of earth. They serve to remind us that the universe and man who dwells therein are encompassed on all sides by the powers and the providences, the graces and the blessings of the Divine; they are part of the Eternal Covenant that He has given His Angels charge over all those who work for the Hidden Wisdom and follow the Quest of Him.*

The Hierophant resumes his seat. The Kerux comes forward and hands the Fylfot Cross to the Hierophant.

Hierophant: *The Hermetic or Fylfot Cross is a great astronomical symbol which speaks to those who can interpret concerning concerning the Divine in the universe. It is formed of 17 squares extracted in a peculiar manner from a square of 25 squares. Observe that the Sun is in the centre and that it is surrounded by the four elements and the twelve zodiacal signs. You also are a centre in the universe; let your light shine before it. You are a centre of your own system; let the light of your consciousness be poured over your elements, over the parts of your personality, over your seals and characters and signs. As a memorial that you have left the darkness, that you look for the sun of justice to rise in your soul, the veils have been removed from the lights on the summits of the two Pillars.*

A pause.

Hierophant: Frater Kerux, *you have my commands to conduct the* Zelator *from the Temple, which he will afterwards re-enter amidst the symbolism of another stage of his progress.*

The Kerux leads the Neophyte to the door. The Kerux and Neophyte (who is prompted) give the Sign of the Grade, and they leave the Temple. The Kerux returns immediately.

Here ends the First Point.

### *The Second Point*

The arrangement of the Temple is shown in the Official Diagram.

Hierophant—⅂—: Fratres et Sorores, *having been reminded of whence he came and whither he returns, our beloved Neophyte and Postulant for Advancement in this Grade has left the Temple, and he will find it transformed on his return, as if to a place of external religion, a Holy Place, with a Holy of Holies beyond it, behind which there is an inner religion, but its mysteries are not communicated to him in this Grade. . . . Honourable* Frater Hegemon, *may God be with you for ever. Assume your ministries of mercy, in the performance of which you represent in the world of Assiah the glorious loving-kindness and benignity descending from the Supreme Crown through the unmanifest and manifest worlds.*

The Hegemon rises in his place and makes the Sign of the Grade.

Hegemon: *I will take unto me the strength of the Eagle; I will unfold the wings of the Dove; and all who desire in their hearts the graces and lights which abide in the Holy Place, I will bring unto the Mercy-Seat and the rest of the Eternal Sabbath.*

The Hegemon leaves the Temple.

Hierophant: Frater Kerux, *when the Neophyte, under gracious guidance, gives the symbolical battery of the Grade, signifying his obedience to the Law, you will admit him according to form.* Fratres Stolistes et Dadouchos, *follow with your mystic vessels and perform your holy part in the consecration of the Neophyte for the last time in the solemn ceremonies of the Temple.*

The Kerux rises in his place. The Stolistes joins the Dadouchos in the South, and they proceed together to the West, where they follow the Kerux to the door. The battery being given as follows:—1111 111 111—the Kerux opens the door.

Hierophant: Frater Adveniat Regnum (vel alius), *you were admitted in the Grade of Neophyte through the Portal of a Holy House, typically represented by that place of God which was built of old in Israel. You came already into the precincts thereof, even into the Court of the Tabernacle, where stood the Altar of Burnt Offerings, on which animals were immolated in sacrifice. It is an image of that greater Altar whereupon the Archangel Michael sacrifices the souls of the just.*

The Dadouchos makes a Cross with his Thurible in front of the Neophyte and censes thrice.

Dadouchos: *When his earthly part has been burnt to ashes, the spirit of man shall ascend, as the sparks fly upward.*

Hierophant: *Between the Altar of Burnt Offerings and the entrance to the Holy Place stood the Laver of Brass, wherein the priests washed before they entered the Tabernacle. It was a symbol of the Waters of Creation. Remember, O*

Frater, *that through the fires and waters of this earthly life
we are prepared for the things that are of heaven.*

The Stolistes marks the Neophyte with a Cross on his forehead
and sprinkles thrice.

Stolistes: *Purify the earthly part, O Lord: purge away the old
leaven: sanctify the acts of man.*

The Hegemon returns to his seat and the Kerux takes charge of
the Candidate.

Hierophant: *Having made his offering at the Altar of Burnt Sacrifice, having been cleansed in the Laver of Brass, the Priest
then entered the Holy Place. From earthly into spiritual life,
from the places of lesser purification, come into the place
that is holy; enter into the presence of God.*

The Kerux stations the Neophyte at a short distance behind the
Pillars with his face to the East. The Stolistes and Dadouchos
return to their seats. The Hiereus proceeds with the sun round
the Black Pillar, and stands between the Pillars, facing the Neophyte, guarding the Path with his Sword.

Hiereus: *Purified in the earthly part, consecrated in the manifest
body, O Neophyte of the ∴ ∴, give me the signs of the Neophyte. They are the title of your passage through the gate.*

The Signs are given. The Hiereus returns to his Throne. The
Kerux leads the Candidate between the Pillars. The Hegemon,
coming forward, stands East of the Pillars and bars the way of
progress with his Sceptre.

Hegemon: *I come from the Mercy-Seat; I come in the Name of the
Light. You who are zealous of the Light, you whom I will
lead into its glory, show me the warrants that you bring;
give me the Sign of a Zelator.*

It is given accordingly. The Hegemon draws the Neophyte
between the Pillars. The Kerux returns to his seat.

Hegemon: *I will lead you, I will bring you, into the House of Light.*

The Hegemon takes the Zelator to the North.

Hegemon: *The Table of Shewbread stood on the Northern side of the Holy Place, and the Twelve Loaves placed thereon were emblematic of the Bread of Life. Some part of its secret meaning is shown in the diagram before you. The 12 external circles represent the mystic loaves, and the Lamp in the centre is the grace and life and light by which the material nourishment of man may be changed into the food of souls: it is the power behind the Sacraments. In another sense the diagram represents the Rose of Creation, the universe of manifested things and the Divine Immanence which abides like a secret light within it. The 12 circles are referred to the 12 simple letters of the Hebrew alphabet, and these also typify the Divine Elements by which all creation is permeated. They signify further the 12 directions of space, the 12 constellations of the Zodiac, the 12 permutations of the Sacred Name of God and the 12 tribes of Israel, representing those who have been called and chosen, out of all tribes and tongues and peoples and nations, for the mystic work in the world. Finally, the circles compose the crown of 12 stars on the head of* **Adonai Malkah,** *the Mother in manifestation, ruling in her kingdom of* **Malkuth.** *They are the outer petals of the Rose. Within the 12 circles are 4 interior circles, containing the Kerubic emblems—the Lion, the Man, the Bull and the Eagle, which are in correspondence with the 4 parts of our natural personality. In this sense the Lamp, standing on the Pentagram, represents their transmutation and quintessence. You should understand in conclusion that, the explanation of every thing being within and not without us, the Rose of Creation is also the Rose of our humanity, and the Lamp in the centre of the diagram is the higher consciousness. Man is thus the explanation of every thing, and the key to this mystery is that God is within.*

The Hegemon takes the Zelator to the South, where he is joined by the Hiereus. The Hegemon resumes his seat.

Hiereus: *The Seven-branched Candlestick stood on the Southern side of the Holy Place, and it is represented here in a diagram by the mystic star of the Heptagram. It is in correspondence with the Seven Palaces of Assiah, or the material world, and with the seven double letters, signifying the Divine efficacy therein, by which the Palaces of Assiah become the Holy Place. This place is the glorious Palace of Holiness, represented by the Lamp in the centre. The Seven-branched Candlestick is also in analogy with the Seven Churches of Asia, and even as the branches of the light-bearer are bound together, springing from one root and one stem, so are the Seven Churches one Holy Church of the Elect. And as the Angels of the Churches are Stars for the enlightenment thereof, so is there a mystic lesson in the seven planets and in the days of the week. For the days are like Seven Churches, and it is yours, O Elect* Frater, *through the week of your earthly life, so to consecrate and rule your life within them that they shall be one Church and one most Holy Temple, with God dwelling therein. Thus shall you deserve to be crowned at the end of all with that chaplet of Seven Stars which are the gift of the Spirit.*

The Hiereus conducts the Zelator to the West of the Altar, whither the Hierophant comes. The Hiereus returns to his seat. The Dadouchos lifts up his Thurible, which is taken by the Hierophant, who makes a Cross in the air therewith and offers incense thrice.

Hierophant (at the first censing): *Glory be to God, Who is declared in the heart of man to those who are pure in heart.* (At the second censing.) *Glory be to God, Who is manifested in the light of created things.* (At the third censing.) *Glory be to God in the Transcendance, in the place of concealed mystery. We adore Thee in the presence of the veil. O take us in Thine own good time, Thy gracious and saving time, beyond all veils, behind Thy palms and pomegranates, into the Holy of Holies.*

A pause.

Hierophant: *Before the Veil of the Holy of Holies stood the golden Altar of Incense, of which this is an image. It stands in the middle place of our Temple and is in the form of a double cube, presenting the surface of things to the eye of sense but concealing the root and the source, as He is concealed in the universe Who is Author and Cause of all. The Altar of Incense was gold because of the Quintessence, but this altar is black because of the corruptible elements from which the Quintessence is extracted, because of the Divine Darkness, because we await transmutation, and because the witness of Nature to Grace is a witness in the night of time. Upon the Cubical Altar were Fire, Water and Incense, corresponding to* Aleph, Mem *and* Shin, *the three Mother letters of the Hebrew alphabet. The divisions of this alphabet, of which you have heard briefly in connection with the Table of Shewbread, the Seven-branched Candlestick and the Altar of Incense, are but a part of the deep symbolism which lies behind the letters of the word of man—itself a shadow and reflection of that Eternal Word which is concealed everywhere, but is declared in the secret heart. From the throne of your imperishable spirit,* O Frater Adveniat Regnum (vel alius), *may the Triad and the Unity therein look forth upon the Kingdom which is yours; may the seven spirits and the seven graces encircle it; and may the twelve fruits of the Tree of Life ripen in your external part.*

The Hierophant returns to his Throne, the Zelator remaining at the Altar.

Hierophant: *I now confer on you the Mystical Title of* Pereclinus de Faustis, *which signifies that on this earth you are as in a wilderness far from the garden of the soul. As it is also the name of those who have come out from the life of earth, seeking the light of the Spirit, I give you the symbol of* Aretz, *which is the Hebrew name of Earth. The word Zelator has been sometimes referred to the ancient Egyptian* Zār' athor, *signifying Searcher of* Athor, *the Goddess of Nature. May you so seek, my brother, that through Nature you shall enter into Grace. May you be worthy of your high calling. May you come with joy and go forth in gladness. May God Himself guide you, if haply our steps fail in the path which leads to the heights.*

The Kerux comes forward and conducts the new Zelator to a seat in the North-East.

Hierophant—𐤟—: Frater Kerux, *lift up your Wand of Office; lift up the Light that you carry; and declare in this Holy Temple that our* Frater Adveniat Regnum (vel alius) *has been advanced to the Grade of* Zelator *and has received, by a regular communication, the titles conferred therein.*

Kerux: *The Name of* Adonai *is before us; The Name of* Malkah *is before us; the Lord of Earth, the Bride and Queen of the Kingdom: Truly Honoured Hierophant, in those names and obeying your high ordinance, I proclaim that* Frater Adveniat Regnum (vel alius) *has been regularly admitted to the 1=10 Grade of* Zelator *and has received the* Mystic Title of Pereclinus de Faustis, *with the symbol of* Aretz.

He salutes the East in passing and returns by West to his seat.

Hierophant: Malkuth *is a place of the darkness, a place of the shadowed light, a place of illumination in Holy and Secret Sanctuaries. The powers and the glories, the mercies also and the graces, through the paths and worlds of the* Sephiroth *above, are sent down therein. It is the first* Sephira *in the way of our return whence we came, and it is therefore called 1 in our system. But seeing that on the outward path, by which the spirit of man travelled into manifestation, it is the tenth and last* Sephira, *so also its number is 10, and it is in this sense that the Grade to which you have been advanced is described as 1=10. As it is a path which takes into manifestation, so it is a gate which leads therefrom. It is therefore termed* Shaar, *which signifies gate, and this word produces by metathesis another word* Oshr, *which signifies the number 10. In* Chaldaic *a gate is* Throa, *the numeration of which is identical with the Holy Name* Adonai, *when the latter is written at full length.*

*The Tenth Path of the* Sepher Yetzirah, *or Kabalistic Book of Formation, is referred to the* Sephira Malkuth *and is termed the Resplendent Intelligence, because it is exalted above every head and is enthroned finally in* Binah, *or the sphere of Supernal Understanding. It is the root and the fountain of light, the splendour of all illumination, and thence is derived that Divine Influence which descends from the Prince of Countenances, the Great Angel* Metatron.

A pause.

Hierophant: Frater Adveniat Regnum (vel alius), *your title to further advancement in the Grades of the Order will continue to depend upon the maintenance of the Holy Fire which your aspiration has enkindled within you. Guard therefore that fire, as we on our side will guard your memory in our hearts; and be sure that when you come again to our Temple, carrying the proper warrants, asking in humility and reverence for tidings of the Holy of Holies, we shall hear your voice, and when you knock we shall surely answer.*

Here ends the Second Point.

The Allocution of the Grade follows, and may be delivered by the Hierophant or one of the Wardens of the Temple.

## *The Allocution of the Grade of Zelator*

Fratres et Sorores, *by the faithful witnesses whose counsels have been transmitted from of old, we know that the Tree of Life is united to the Supernals in* Daath. *In some high region of the mind, above the disctinctions which obtain between good and evil, and merged in the absolute goodness which fills the soul entirely, there is an union which the soul attains, so that knowl-*

*edge is on all sides, and is infinite and holy. I invite you, therefore, to hear in the repose and the stillness which follow each stage of activity, marking our progress in the work, the Allocution belonging to the Grade of Zelator. And you, our Postulant, who have this day crossed that threshold to which you were brought only in the previous degree, I solicit and claim your attention to a few salutary inferences which should be taken away from the experience through which you have just passed, being that of the advancement which follows reception into the House of Our Order. Here, as in other departments of intellectual and spiritual life, advancement is in virtue of knowledge extended slowly. It corresponds to the partial communication of that light which in the Grade of Neophyte we desire may be extended to the Postulant and increased within him. He is now pictured as having reached the outer side of that Portal which is called Wisdom, and if it be only in symbolism that he has earned the title for it to be opened at his knocking, he is still instructed to knock, and what follows is that it does open. He enters amidst the harmonious rumours which move about the building of the Mystic House and of the Spiritual City; his face is set towards the East, as one who should see Zion on the sacred hill when the Orient from on high has flooded it, when the night and its shadows are over. But the Postulant for the Grade of Neophyte comes in darkness to the threshold and in the Court of the Holy Temple his eyes are opened for a period. They close again in the Grade of Zelator, because of the unknown heights, but it is for a moment only, and again they are now opened. Let us pray that for him and those who are like him all folds and scales and bandages may fall from the inward eyes and that there shall be no more darkness within.*

*The symbolic experience through which the Postulant passes in this Grade is that of the middle path, as between good and evil or light and shadow. The Angel of the Evil Path, as the protector against that evil which is within him, has told him that he shall not pass by, for his own pledges forbid him. But the Angel of the Perfect Path tells him that he cannot proceed, seeing that he enter only in the likeness of the natural man, as yet unquali-*

*fied further. That which is open to him is therefore the Path of Equilibrium, and it takes him to the East, which symbolises spiritual knowledge. Thence the Postulant looks, from his base on this earth, towards the City which is beyond, or the House of his desire, and he sees the great distance stretching before him— an immeasurable distance which he is prepared to enter. He knows also, or may at least divine it, if he have brought within the circle of our Order something of the light of thought, that distances of themselves are nothing, nor do places signify, because that which we reach in the height is already here. There are no greater opportunities than those of to-day; there are no hindrances so insuperable that will and desire cannot in their transmutation, and with their changing power, convert them into perfect paths. When, therefore, the Postulant looks toward the East of the Temple, when the voice of the Hierophant speaks to him of Great Mysteries, of the Tree and the Garden, he knows that these things are also here and now, that Malkuth is the Kingdom, that the Kingdom is also a Garden and the Paradise that is below, while the Tree is not separable from these.* Fratres et Sorores, *here is the way of the Tree of Life, now is the call thereto, and if some swords are broken at the entrance-gate, if for some the Sword of the* Kerubim *keep that way too keenly, there is also a Sword of the Spirit, before which even the* Kerubim *raise their guard, so that those who are born for the Sanctuary may enter and go in. Here ends the First Point.*

*The symbolism has changed in the Second from that of the Garden of Eden to the Mysteries of the Holy Place, of the Spiritual House manifested on this earth—this earth enlightened by a material sun, itself the sphere of the elements, encircled by the belt of the Zodiac. For the earth is the gate of the Holy Place, and the Holy of Holies is manifested therein for those who are qualified to enter. Whether we are conscious or not of His Divine Presence, the Reconciler is always with us, speaking from the Mercy-Seat and preparing the way to the Celestial Light. In such a Temple, my brethren—at once manifest and concealed—you are the burnt offerings; you are also the altar; it is by the sacrifice of your proper selves, and so only, as in a great purgation and cleansing, that you can enter truly and essentially the Holy Place which you have now entered symbolically. There is the Bread of Life, which is shown in our symbolism to correspond with the whole of creation, because God nourishes His children, substantially and supersubstantially, on all the planes, and the high angels, which guard the inmost precincts of the Mysteries, do communicate—to those who can receive—the Food of Souls, in every region of the universe. In that Temple also are held, as if in archives, the hidden doctrines of the Divine Mystery, leading by steep paths to the Crown and Quintessence of all Experience in the term of sanctity. But you should note that it is out of the corruptible earth that the true Quintessence is extracted, showing that the way of your election—the path of life to which and in which it has pleased God to call you—is for you the nearest way. After this manner does the mystic Temple contain all things symbolically. But* Malkuth *is also the Temple, and the Mystery of the Tenth Path, about which you have just heard, shows that* Malkuth *is understood after more than one manner, because that which is begun on earth is completed in Heaven. There is, lastly, a certain state of mind by which an intelligence that is other than the logical understanding—which is more resplendent and more highly enthroned—descends through an ordered channel, as a light of the Prince of Countenances. And this channel is that Path by which the* Zelator *goes up.*

If the Minutes of any previous Meeting or other official business are to be taken in the Grade of Zelator, the Temple must be reduced at this point to the Grade of Neophyte. By the power of his Sceptre, the Hierophant must close in the higher Grade, open in the lower, and, after the business has been completed, must close therein and reopen in the Grade of Zelator.

### The Solemn Office of Closing the Sacred Temple in the Grade of Zelator

The Sentinel having left the Temple:

Hierophant—ו—

All rise.

Hierophant: Fratres et Sorores Zelatores, *I beseech you to assist me with one mind in the closing of the heart against the world.*

Hiereus: *Truly Honoured Hierophant, I testify on behalf of the Brethren, I testify on my own part, that the heart is guarded.*

Hierophant: *Let that which is watched within, even in the sacred precincts, be protected also beyond, in the world to which we return. . . . Frater Kerux, remembering the correspondence between things within and without, I direct you to see that the Temple is properly secured.*

The Kerux knocks once on the inner side of the Portal, and is answered after the same manner by the Sentinel without.

Kerux: *Truly Honoured Hierophant, that which is symbolised on the hither side of the Portal is reflected on the further side by diligent, external guarding.*

Hierophant: *The earth is full of His goodness; the pillars of the earth are the Lord's; the earth is full of His riches: let us adore the Lord and King of Earth.*

The Hierophant descends from his Throne and faces East. He extends his Sceptre on high in the Sign of the Grade. All face East and maintain the Sign.

Hierophant: Adonai-Ha-Aretz, Adonai Malkah; *we have desired Thee in all generations. Spirit of the Lord, say: Come; Bride of the Lord, say: Come. We have watched in the night because of Thee: we have worked in the day because of Thee:*

*we die in the endurance of our longing: make us alive in Thee. O earth, earth, earth; part of the earth in us; hear the Word of the Lord. Amen.*

The Hierophant passes to the North, and pauses before the Tablet of the North. All face to that point. The Hiereus takes up his place at the right of the Hierophant and the Hegemon on his left hand. The Kerux stands behind the Hierophant, the Stolistes behind the Hegemon and the Dadouchos behind the Hiereus, carrying their respective implements of Office.

Hierophant: *Let us offer the mystic prayer of the Earth-spirits, typifying the powers and activities of our own material part, aspiring towards the Great Master.*—⅂—

### The Prayer of the Spirits of Earth

*O King Invisible, Who, taking the Earth for a foundation, didst hollow its depths to fill them with Thine Almighty Power! Thou Whose Name shaketh the Arches of the World; Thou Who causest the seven metals to flow in the veins of the rocks; King of the Seven Lights; Rewarder of the subterranean workers; lead us into the desirable air, into the realm of splendour. We watch and we labour unceasingly; we seek and we hope; by the Twelve Stones of the Holy City; by the Buried Talismans; by the axis of loadstone which passes through the centre of the earth! O Lord! O Lord! O Lord! Have pity on those who suffer, expand our hearts, unbind and upraise our minds, enlarge our natures! O Stability and Motion! O Day clothed with Night! O Darkness veiled by Splendour! O Master, Who never dost withhold the wages of Thy workers! O Silver Whiteness! O Golden Splendour! O Crown of Living and Melodious Diamonds! Thou Who wearest the Heaven on Thy finger as a sapphire ring; Thou Who concealest under the earth, in the kingdom of precious stones, the marvellous seed of stars; Live; Reign; and Be Thou the Eternal Dispenser of the treasures whereof Thou hast made us the Wardens. Amen.*

The Hierophant makes the Banishing Pentagram of Earth.

Hierophant: *Depart in the peace of the Everlasting; depart to your proper places, your paths and grades and activities. The graces and benedictions of* Adonai *be upon you, and be you ready for the call of His service.*

All Officers return to their places and all face as usual.

Hierophant: *Our hearts are licensed to go forth into the outer world, carrying the memorials of the covenants made within. In the name of* Adonai, *I declare this Temple closed in the Grade of Zeal and Aspiration.*

Hierophant—꜀꜀꜀꜀ ꜀꜀꜀ ꜀꜀꜀—

Hiereus—꜀꜀꜀꜀ ꜀꜀꜀ ꜀꜀꜀—

Hegemon—꜀꜀꜀꜀ ꜀꜀꜀ ꜀꜀꜀—

Here ends the Ritual of the Grade of Zelator.

# Bibliography

Bullinger, Ethelbert W. *Witness of the Stars*. Grand Rapids, MI: Kregel Publications, 1972.

Jung, C. G. *Mysterium Coniunctionis*. Princeton, NJ: Princeton University Press, 1970.

le Plongeon, Augustus. *Sacred Mysteries Among the Mayans and the Quiches*. San Diego, CA: Wizards Bookshelf, 1973 (original ed. 1886).

*Lost Books of the Bible & the Forgotten Books of Eden*. New York: New American Library, 1948.

Regardie, Israel. *The Golden Dawn*. St. Paul, MN: Llewellyn Publications, Inc., 6th ed., 1989.

Regardie, Israel. *The Complete Golden Dawn System of Magic*. Phoenix, AZ: Falcon Press, 1984.

Zalewski, Patrick J. *Secret Inner Order Rituals of the Golden Dawn*. Phoenix, AZ: Falcon Press, 1988.

Zalewski, Pat. *Golden Dawn Enochian Magic.* St. Paul, MN: Llewellyn Publications, Inc., 1990.

Zalewski, Pat. *Z-5: Secret Teachings of the Golden Dawn—Book I: The Neophyte Ritual 0=0.* St. Paul, MN: Llewellyn Publications, Inc., 1991.

## STAY IN TOUCH

On the following pages you will find listed, with their current prices, some of the books now available on related subjects. Your book dealer stocks most of these, and will stock new titles in the Llewellyn series as they become available. We urge your patronage.

However, to obtain our full catalog, to keep informed of new titles as they are released and to benefit from informative articles and helpful news, you are invited to write for our bi-monthly news magazine/catalog. A sample copy is free, and it will continue coming to you at no cost as long as you are an active mail customer. Or you may keep it coming for a full year with a donation of just $5.00 in U.S.A. & Canada ($20.00 overseas, first class mail). Many bookstores also have *The Llewellyn New Times* available to their customers. Ask for it.

Stay in touch! In *The Llewellyn New Times'* pages you will find news and reviews of new books, tapes and services, announcements of meetings and seminars, articles helpful to our readers, news of authors, advertising of products and services, special money-making opportunities, and much more.

### *The Llewellyn New Times*
**P.O. Box 64383-Dept. 896, St. Paul, MN 55164-0383, U.S.A.**
● ● ●
## TO ORDER BOOKS AND TAPES

If your book dealer does not have the books described on the following pages readily available, you may order them direct from the publisher by sending full price in U.S. funds, plus $1.50 for postage and handling for orders *under* $10.00; $3.00 for orders *over* $10.00. There are no postage and handling charges for orders over $50. UPS Delivery: We ship UPS whenever possible. Delivery guaranteed. Provide your street address as UPS does not deliver to P.O. Boxes. UPS to Canada requires a $50 minimum order. Allow 4–6 weeks for delivery. Orders outside the U.S.A. and Canada: Airmail—add retail price of book; add $5 for each non-book item (tapes, etc.); add $1 per item for surface mail.

## FOR GROUP STUDY AND PURCHASE

Because there is a great deal of interest in group discussion and study of the subject matter of this book, we feel that we should encourage the adoption and use of this particular book by such groups by offering a special "quantity" price to group leaders or "agents."

Our Special Quantity Price for a minimum order of five copies of *Z-5: Secret Teachings of the Golden Dawn (Book II: The Zelator Ritual 1=10)* is $38.85 cash-with-order. This price includes postage and handling within the United States. Minnesota residents must add 6.5% sales tax. For additional quantities, please order in multiples of five. For Canadian and foreign orders, add postage and handling charges as above. Credit card (VISA, Master Card, American Express) orders are accepted. Charge card orders only may be phoned free ($15.00 minimum order) within the U.S.A. or Canada by dialing 1-800-THE-MOON. Customer service calls dial 1-612-291-1970. Mail Orders to:

### LLEWELLYN PUBLICATIONS
**P.O. Box 64383-Dept. 896, St. Paul, MN 55164-0383, U.S.A.**

Prices subject to change without notice.

## Z–5—SECRET TEACHINGS OF THE GOLDEN DAWN
## BOOK I: THE NEOPHYTE RITUAL 0=0
**by Pat Zalewski**

This book is the first in a series on the grade rituals of the Hermetic Order of the Golden Dawn. It is designed to show the type of procedure one encounters when he or she joins a Golden Dawn temple. It focuses on the secret, Inner Order techniques for performing the Neophyte initiation ritual, which is the essence of the Golden Dawn's Z–2 magical instructions.

Z–5 is a tool and a helpful guide based on the observations of a number of Adepts from the Golden Dawn, the Stella Matutina, and the Smaragdum Thalasses. Originally intended as a document restricted to members of the Inner Order of the Thoth-Hermes Temple, the Z–5 material includes many of the "word of mouth" teachings passed on from Inner Order Adepti. These teachings go beyond the step-by-step mechanics of ritual on the mundane level and unveil the *deeper* meanings, allowing access into the Golden Dawn's "magical current," is the source of the true power of ritual.

0–87542–897–5, 229 pgs., 6 x 9, illus., softcover                     $12.95

## THE EQUINOX & SOLSTICE CEREMONIES
## OF THE GOLDEN DAWN
**by Pat & Chris Zalewski**

Throughout time, the Spring and Fall Equinoxes and Summer and Winter Solstices have been the basic reference points for the seasons and the major times for celebration in both the Christian and Pagan calendars. Yet until now, there has been little in the way of detailed information on the *magical effects* of the Equinox and Solstice.

*The Equinox & Solstice Ceremonies of the Golden Dawn* is a valuable contribution to magical literature. It defines and explains the Equinox and Solstice, along with the Golden Dawn concept of them. It presents a scientific evaluation of the magnetic fields they produce, along with the astrological data connecting them and how they relate to spiritual development. It investigates myths and festivals from the time of the Egyptians and how the theology of that time related specifically to the Sun and the change of the seasons. Jewish, Christian, Celtic and Norse festivals are also explored along with the different timing of these ceremonies in different climatic conditions. The authors then present the full Golden Dawn rituals and give their expert commentary, which reveals many unpublished teachings associated with the ceremonies.

0–87542–899–1, 192 pgs., 6 x 9, illus., softcover                     $12.95

## GOLDEN DAWN ENOCHIAN MAGIC
### by Pat Zalewski

Enochian magic is considered by most magicians to be the most powerful system ever created. Aleister Crowley, "The Great Beast," learned this system of magic from the Hermetic Order of the Golden Dawn, which had developed and expanded the concepts and discoveries of Elizabethan magus John Dee. This book picks up where the published versions of the Enochian material of the Golden Dawn leave off.

Based on the research and unpublished papers of MacGregor Mathers, one of the founders of the Golden Dawn, *Golden Dawn Enochian Magic* opens new avenues of use for this system. New insights are given on such topics as the Sigillum Dei Aemeth, the Angels of the Enochian Aires applied to the 12 tribes of Israel and the Kabbalah, the 91 Governors, the Elemental Tablets as applied to the celestial sphere, and more. This book provides a long-sought break from amateurish and inaccurate books on the subject; it is designed to complement such scholarly classics as *Enochian Invocation* and *Heptarchia Mystica*.

0-87542-898-3, 224 pgs., 6 x 9, illus., softcover                    $12.95

## THE GOLDEN DAWN
### by Israel Regardie

The Original Account of the Teachings, Rites and Ceremonies of the Hermetic Order of the Golden Dawn as revealed by Israel Regardie, with further revision, expansion, and additional notes by Regardie, Cris Monnastre, and others. Expanded with an index of more than 100 pages!

Originally published in four bulky volumes of some 1200 pages, this 6th Revised and Enlarged Edition has been entirely reset in modern, less space-consuming type, in half the pages (while retaining the original pagination in marginal notation for reference) for greater ease and use.

Also included are Initiation Ceremonies, important rituals for consecration and invocation, methods of meditation and magical working based on the Enochian Tablets, studies in the Tarot, and the system of Qabalistic Correspondences that unite the World's religions and magical traditions into a comprehensive and practical whole.

This volume is designed as a study and practice curriculum suited to both group and private practice. Meditation upon, and following with the Active Imagination, the Initiation Ceremonies is fully experiential without need of participation in group or lodge. A very complete reference encyclopedia of Western Magick.

0-87542-663-8, 840 pgs., 6 x 9, illus., softcover                    $19.95

## THE MIDDLE PILLAR
### by Israel Regardie

Between the two outer pillars of the Qabalistic Tree of Life, the extremes of Mercy and Severity, stands THE MIDDLE PILLAR, signifying one who has achieved equilibrium in his or her own self.

Integration of the human personality is vital to the continuance of creative life. Without it, man lives as an outsider to his own true self. By combining Magic and Psychology in the Middle Pillar Ritual/Exercise (a magical meditation technique),we bring into balance the opposing elements of the psyche while yet holding within their essence and allowing full expression of man's entire being.

In this book, and with this practice, you will learn to: understand the psyche through its correspondences on the Tree of Life; expand self-awareness, thereby intensifying the inner growth process; activate creative and intuitive potentials; understand the individual thought patterns which control every facet of personal behavior; regain the sense of balance and peace of mind—the equilibrium that everyone needs for physical and psychic health.

0–87542–658–1, 176 pgs., 5-1/4 x 8, softcover      $8.95


## A GARDEN OF POMEGRANATES
### by Israel Regardie

What is the Tree of Life? It's the ground plan of the Qabalistic system—a set of symbols used since ancient times to study the Universe. The Tree of Life is a geometrical arrangement of ten sephiroth, or spheres, each of which is associated with a different archetypal idea, and 22 paths which connect the spheres.

This system of primal correspondences has been found the most efficient plan ever devised to classify and organize the characteristics of the self. Israel Regardie has written one of the best and most lucid introductions to the Qabalah.

*A Garden of Pomegranates* combines Regardie's own studies with his notes on the works of Aleister Crowley, A. E. Waite, Eliphas Levi and D. H. Lawrence. No longer is the wisdom of the Qabalah to be held secret! The needs of today place the burden of growth upon each and every person— each has to undertake the Path as his or her own responsibility, but every help is given in the most ancient and yet most modern teaching here known to humankind.

0–87542–690–5, 160 pgs., 5-1/4 x 8, softcover      $8.95

## ATTAINMENT THROUGH MAGIC
### by William G. Gray

In this newly titled re-release of the classic *A Self Made by Magic*, the author presents a "Self-Seeking System" of powerful magical practice designed to help seekers become better and more fulfilled souls. The source material is taken from standard procedures familiar to most students of the Western Inner Tradition, procedures that encourage the best of our potential while-diminishing or eliminating our worst characteristics. To that end, Gray deals extensively with the dangers and detriments of maleficent or "black" magic.

The lessons follow the pattern of the Life-Tree, and guide the student through the four elements and their connection of Truth, the Ten Principles of "Spheres" of the Life-Tree, and the associations which bind these together. Gray includes an in-depth study of the Archangelic concepts with exercises to "make the Archangels come true" for us through the systematic use of appropriate words of power.

0–87542–298–5, 308 pgs., 5-1/4 x 8, illus., softcover                    **$9.95**

## BETWEEN GOOD AND EVIL
### by William G. Gray

If you are seeking Inner Light, read this important new book. *Between Good and Evil* provides new insight that can help you take the forces of Darkness that naturally exist within us and transform them into spiritual light. This book will help you discover how you can deal constructively, rather than destructively, with the unavoidable problem of Evil. Our lives depend on which way we direct our energy—whether we made the Devil in ourselves serve the God, or the other way around. We must use our Good intentions to understand and exploit the Evil energies that would otherwise prove fatal to us.

In order to confront and control our "demons," Gray has revived a centuries-old magical ritual technique called the *Abramelin Experience*: a practical step-by-step process in which you call upon your Holy Guardian Angel to assist in converting Evil into Good. By following the richly detailed explanation of this "spiritual alchemy," you will learn how to positively channel your negative energies into a path leading directly to a re-union with Divinity.

The power of altering your future lies in your own hands, and within this unique book you will discover the means to move forward in your spiritual evolution. You will find the principles discussed in this multifaceted book valuable and insightful.

0–87542–273–X, 272 pgs., 5-1/4x 8, softcover                    **$9.95**

Prices subject to change without notice.

**BY STANDING STONE & ELDER TREE**
**by William G. Gray**
Originally published in 1975 as *The Rollright Ritual*, this book is the re-release of this fascinating work complete with illustrations and a new introduction by the author. The famous stone circle of the "Rollrights" in Oxfordshire, England, is well known to folklorists. Gray, through the use of psychometry, has retrieved the story of the rocks from the rocks themselves—the story of the culture that placed them and the ritual system used by the ancient stone setters.

This book shows how you can create a Rollright Circle anywhere you wish, even in your own backyard, or within your own mind during meditation. Gray provides specific instructions and a script with an explanation of the language. Even for those not interested in performing the ritual, *By Standing Stone & Elder Tree* provides an exciting exploration of ancient cultures and of the value that stones hold for the fate of modern civilization.

0–87542–299–3, 208 pages, 5-1/4 x 8, illus., softcover                    $9.95


**EVOKING THE PRIMAL GODDESS**
**Discovery of the Eternal Feminine Within**
**by William G. Gray**
In our continuing struggle to attain a higher level of spiritual awareness, one thing has become clear: we need to cultivate and restore the matriarchal principle to its proper and equal place in our conceptions of Deity. Human history and destiny are determined by our Deity concepts, whatever they may be, and for too long the results of a predominantly masculine God in war, brutality and violence have been obvious.

In *Evoking the Primal Goddess*, renowned occultist William G. Gray takes you on a fascinating, insightful journey into the history and significance of the Goddess in religion. For the first time anywhere, he shows that the search for the Holy Grail was actually a movement within the Christian church to bring back the feminine element into the concept of Deity. He also shows how you can evoke your own personal image of the Mother ideal through practical rituals and prayer.

It has been said that whatever happens in spiritual levels of life will manifest itself on physical ones as well. By following Gray's techniques, you can rebalance both your male and your female polarities into a single spiritual individuality of practical Power!

0–87542–271–3, 192 pgs., 5-1/4 x 8, photos, softcover                    $9.95

## GROWING THE TREE WITHIN:
### Patterns of the Unconscious Revealed by the Qabalah
### by William G. Gray

The Qabalah, or Tree of Life, has been the basic genetic pattern of Western esotericism, and it shows us mortals how to make our climb steadily back to Heaven. When we study the Qabalah, open ourselves to it and work with it as an Inner Activity, we gain wisdom that will illuminate our individual paths to perfection. Qabalah means "getting wise" in the broadest possible sense.

Formerly titled *The Talking Tree*, this book presents an exhaustive and systematic analysis of the 22 Paths of the Tree of Life. It includes a detailed and comprehensive study of the symbolism of the Tarot cards in which author William Gray presents a viable yet unorthodox method of allocating the Major Arcana to the Paths. Of particular interest is his attempt at reaching a better understanding of the nature of the English alphabet and its correspondence to the Tree of Life.

Gray contends that the "traditional" Tree is a living spirit that needs to be in a continual state of evolution and improvement. It is the duty of all those who love and work with it to cultivate and develop it with every care. This includes both pruning off dead wood and training new growth in the right directions for future fruiting. *Growing the Tree Within* does precisely that.
0–87542–268–3, 468 pgs., 6 x 9, illus., softcover           **$14.95**


## TEMPLE MAGIC
### by William G. Gray

This important book on occultism deals specifically with problems and details you are likely to encounter in temple practice. Learn how a temple should look, how a temple should function, what a ceremonialist should wear, what physical postures best promote the ideal spiritual-mental attitude, and how magic is worked in a temple.

*Temple Magic* has been written specifically for the instruction and guidance of esoteric ceremonialists by someone who has spent a lifetime in spiritual service to his natural Inner Way. There are few comparable works in existence, and this book in particular deals with up-to-date techniques of constructing and using a workable temple dedicated to the furtherance of the Western Inner Tradition. In simple yet adequate language, it helps any individual understand and promote the spiritual structure of our esoteric inheritance. It is a book by a specialist for those who are intending to be specialists.
0–87542–274–8, 288 pgs., 5-1/4 x 8, illus., softcover         **$7.95**


Prices subject to change without notice.

**EARTH GOD RISING**
**The Return of the Male Mysteries**
**by Alan Richardson**
Today, in an age that is witnessing the return of the Goddess in all ways
and on all levels, the idea of one more male deity may appear to be a step
backward. But along with looking toward the feminine powers as a cure for
our personal and social ills, we must remember to invoke those forgotten
and positive aspects of out most ancient God. The Horned God is just,
never cruel; firm, but not vindictive. The Horned God loves women as
equals. He provides the balance needed in this New Age, and he must be
invoked as clearly and as ardently as the Goddess to whom he is twin.

The how-to section of this book shows how to make direct contact with
your most ancient potentials, as exemplified by the Goddess and the
Horned God. Using the simplest of techniques, available to everyone in
any circumstance, *Earth God Rising* shows how we can create our own mystery and bring about real magical transformations without the need for
groups, gurus, or elaborate ceremonies.

0–87542–672–7, 256 pgs., 5-1/4 x 8, illus., softcover                      **$9.95**


**20TH CENTURY MAGIC AND THE OLD RELIGION:**
**Dion Fortune, Christine Hartley, Charles Seymour**
**by Alan Richardson**
This magical record details the work of two senior magicians—Charles
Seymour and Christine Hartley—within Dion Fortune's Society of the In-
ner Light during the years 1937 to 1939.

Using juxtaposed excerpts from Seymour and Hartley's magical diaries together with biographical prefaces containing unique insights into the background and nature of the Society, Alan Richardson paints a fascinating picture of Dion Fortune and her fellow adepts at the peak of their magical ca-
reers.

Originally published as *Dancers to the Gods*, now with a new introduction
and the addition of Seymour's long essay, "The Old Religion," a manual of
self-initiation, this new edition retains Dion Fortune's "lost" novels, the
past-life identities of her Secret Chiefs, and much more.

The simple act of reading these juxtaposed diaries of a true priest and
priestess can cause a resonance with the soul which will ultimately transform those who so desire it.

0–87542–673–5, 288 pgs., 6 x 9, photos, softcover                      **$12.95**

Prices subject to change without notice.

## ANCIENT MAGICKS FOR A NEW AGE
### by Alan Richardson and Geoff Hughes

With two sets of personal magickal diaries, this book details the work of magicians from two different eras. In it, you can learn what a particular magician is experiencing in this day and age, how to follow a similar path of your own, and discover correlations to the workings of traditional adepti from almost half a century ago.

The first set of diaries are from Christine Hartley and show the magick performed within the Merlin Temple of the Stella Matutina, an offshoot of the Hermetic Order of the Golden Dawn, in the years 1940-42. The second set are from Geoff Hughes, and detail his magickal work during 1984-86. Although he was not at that time a member of any formal group, the magick he practiced was under the same aegis as Hartley's. The third section of this book, written by Hughes, shows how you can become your own Priest or Priestess and make contact with Merlin.

The magick of Christine Hartley and Geoff Hughes are like the poles of some hidden battery that lies beneath the Earth and beneath the years. There is a current flowing between them, and the energy is there for you to tap.

**0-87542-671-9, 320 pgs., 6 x 9, illus., softcover**                                    **$12.95**


## MAGIC AND THE WESTERN MIND
### by Gareth Knight

*Magic and the Western Mind* explains why intelligent and responsible people are turning to magic and the occult as a radical and important way to find meaning in modern life, as well as a means of survival for themselves and the planet.

First published in 1978 as *A History of White Magic*, this book illustrates, in a wide historical survey, how the higher imagination has been used to aid the evolution of consciousness—from the ancient mystery religions, through alchemy, Renaissance magic, the Rosicrucian Manifestoes, Freemasonry, 19th-century magic fraternities, up to psychoanalysis and the current occult revival. Plus it offers some surprising insights into the little-known interests of famous people.

The Western mind developed magic originally as one of the noblest of arts and sciences. Now, with the help of this book, anyone can defend a belief in magic in convincing terms.

**0-87542-374-4, 336 pgs., 6 x 9, illus., softcover**                                    **$12.95**

**SECRETS OF THE GERMAN SEX MAGICIANS**
**A Practical Handbook for Men & Women**
**by Frater U∴ D∴**
*Secrets of the German Sex Magicians* is an introduction to one of the oldest disciplines of a secret lore. It is a complete system of sex magick, in theory and practice—with exercises to develop related abilities for visualization, concentration, breath control, psychic energy arousal and flow. It discusses the fundamental principles in an open manner and with lack of prejudice. The dangers of sex magic and suitable protection measures are also carefully considered.

General interest in this branch of magic is still increasing, yet this may be the only practical introduction to the subject available. This book also differs from the others because, instead of the traditional male orientation, it regards men and women as having equal rights and status.

For the sex magician, the sexual power is first of all a neutral energy, to be directed magically for any purpose. Experience shows that it is very suitable for "success-magic": charging talismans, amulets and sigils, and the achievement of professional, material and psychological advantages.

0–87542–773–1, 240 pgs., 6 x 9, illus., softcover                           $17.95


**PRACTICAL SIGIL MAGIC**
**by Frater U∴ D∴**
This powerful magical system is right for anyone who has the desire to change his/her life! Frater U∴D∴ shows you how to create personal sigils (signs) using your unconscious. Artistic skill is not a necessity in drawing sigils, but honest, straightforward, precise intentions are, and this book gives samples of various sigils along with their purpose.

Based on Austin Osman Spare's theory of sigils and the Alphabet of Desire, *Practical Sigil Magic* explores the background of this magical practice as well as specific methods, such as the word method with its sentence of desire. The pictorial and mantrical spell methods are also explained with many illustrations. The last chapter is devoted solely to creating sigils from planetary cameas.

Once you've created your sigil, you'll learn how to internalize or activate it, finally banishing it from your consciousness as it works imperceptibly in the outer world. Let Frater U∴D∴, a leading magician of Germany, take you on this magical journey to the center of your dreams.

0–87542–774–X, 166 pgs., 5-1/4 x 8, illus., softcover                       $8.95


Prices subject to change without notice.

## NORTHERN MAGIC: Mysteries of the Norse, Germans & English
### by Edred Thorsson

This in-depth primer of the magic of the Northern Way introduces the major concepts and practices of Gothic or Germanic magic. English, German, Dutch, Icelandic, Danish, Norwegian, and Swedish peoples are all directly descended from this ancient Germanic cultural stock. According to author Edred Thorsson, if you are interested in living a holistic life with unity of body-mind-spirit, a key to knowing your spiritual heritage is found in the heritage of your body—in the genetic code which you have inherited from your distant ancestors. Most readers of this book already "speak the language" of the Teutonic tradition.

*Northern Magic* contains material that has never before been discussed in a practical way. This book outlines the ways of Northern magic and the character of the Northern magician. It explores the theories of traditional Northern psychology (or the lore of the soul) in some depth, as well as the religious tradition of the Troth and the whole Germanic theology. The remaining chapters make up a series of "mini-grimoires" on four basic magical techniques in the Northern Way: rune magic, galdor staves, hex signs, and *seith* (or shamanism).

This is an excellent overview of the Teutonic tradition that will interest neophytes as well as long-time travelers along the Northern Way.

**0–87542–782–0, 320 pgs., mass market, illus.**                    **$4.95**

## A KABBALAH FOR THE MODERN WORLD
### by Migene Gonzalez-Wippler

The Kabbalah is the basic form of Western mysticism, and this is an excellent manual of traditional Kabbalistic Magick! It contains one of the best introductions to the Kabbalah ever written.

If you have ever been intimidated by the Kabbalah in the past, and never studied its beauty, this is the book for you. It clearly and plainly explains the complexities of the Kabbalah. This is an ideal book for newcomers to the study of Kabbalah or mysticism and spirituality in general.

*A Kabbalah for the Modern World* is written so clearly that it makes complex kabbalistic ideas easy to understand. This book needs to be in the library of every occultist, Pagan, Kabbalist, and everyone involved in the New Age.

There have been many books over the past several years which have compared psychological theory and the New Age Physics with various Eastern philosophies such as Taoism and Zen. But there is only one which unites psychology, physics and Western mysticism: Migene Gonzalez- Wippler's *A Kabbalah for the Modern World.*

**0-87542-294-2, 256 pgs., 5-1/4 x 8, illus., softcover**                    **$9.95**

Prices subject to change without notice.

## ECSTASY THROUGH TANTRA
### by Dr. Jonn Mumford
Dr. Jonn Mumford makes the occult dimension of the sexual dynamic accessible to everyone. One need not go up to the mountaintop to commune with Divinity: its temple is the body, its sacrament the communion between lovers. *Ecstasy Through Tantra* traces the ancient practices of sex magick through the Egyptian, Greek and Hebrew forms, where the sexual act is viewed as symbolic of the highest union, to the highest expression of Western sex magick.

Dr. Mumford guides the reader through mental and physical exercises aimed at developing psychosexual power; he details the various sexual practices and positions that facilitate "psychic short-circuiting" and the arousal of Kundalini, the Goddess of Life within the body. He shows the fundamental unity of Tantra with Western Wicca, and he plumbs the depths of Western sex magick, showing how its techniques culminate in spiritual illumination.

0–87542–494–5, 190 pgs., 6 x 9, illus., color plates, softcover          $12.95

## SEX MAGICK
### by Louis T. Culling
In sexual union there is a uniting of magnetic and electric currents to create a field of energy that extends both inward and outward to contact the infinite Intelligence and the personal unconscious. In perfecting this union lies Magick, for we gain insight and extend our personal power by becoming a channel to the powers of the universe.

In *Sex Magick* the long hidden secrets and principles of sex magick are revealed with examples that enable one to turn sexual union into a valid tool for mystical ecstasy and self-transcendence.

This is not the magic of sex; *Sex Magick* is using sex as a potent vehicle for magical attainment. Its purpose is to accomplish the mystical union of normal consciousness with the highest consciousness. It embraces a healthy psychological view of man, allowing him to grow and create without restriction. *Sex Magick* is unsurpassed for achieving the highest physical and spiritual ecstasies.

0–87542–110–5, 148 pgs., 5-1/4 x 8, illus., softcover          $6.95

Prices subject to change without notice.

## GODWIN'S CABALISTIC ENCYCLOPEDIA
**by David Godwin**
This is the most complete correlation of Hebrew and English ideas ever offered. It is a dictionary of Cabalism arranged, with definitions, alphabetically, alphabetically in Hebrew, and numerically. With this book the practicing Cabalist or student no longer needs access to a large number of books on mysticism, magic and the occult in order to trace down the basic meanings, Hebrew spellings, and enumerations of the hundreds of terms, words, and names that are included in this book.

This book includes: all of the two-letter root words found in Biblical Hebrew, the many names of God, the Planets, the Astrological Signs, Numerous Angels, the Shem ha-Mephorash, the Spirits of the *Goetia*, the correspondences of the 32 Paths, a comparison of the Tarot and the Cabala, a guide to Hebrew Pronunciation, and a complete edition of Aleister Crowley's valuable book *Sepher Sephiroth*.

Here is a book that is a must for the shelf of all Magicians, Cabalists, Astrologers, Tarot students, Thelemites, and those with any interest at all in the spiritual aspects of our universe.
0-87542-292-6, 528 pgs., 6 x 9, softcover                                $15.00

## LIGHT IN EXTENSION
### Greek Magic from Homer to Modern Times
**by David Godwin**
Greek magic is the foundation of almost every form of ceremonial magic being practiced today. Elements of Greek philosophy summarize the bulk of modern esoteric thought and occult teachings. Even the cabala contains many features that appear to be Greek in origin.

This book explains in plain, informal language the grand sweep of Greek magic and Greek philosophical and religious concepts from the archaic period of Homer's *Iliad* right down to the present. It begins with the magic and mythology of the days of classical Athens and its antecedent cultures, gives detailed considerations of Gnosticism, early Christianity and Neoplatonism—all phenomena with a Greek foundation—explains the manifestations of Greek thought in the Renaissance, and explores modern times with the Greek elements of the magic of the Golden Dawn, Aleister Crowley and others.

From the plains of Troy to the streets of Los Angeles, Greek magic is alive and well. No one who has any interest in magic, occultism, or hermetic thought and who is also a citizen of Western civilization can afford to ignore this heritage.
0-87542-285-3, 272 pgs., 6 x 9, illus., softcover                        $12.95